Birds&Blooms
Beauty in the Backyard

Ruby-throated hummingbird, page 33

Table of Contents

FRONT COVER PHOTO
Dianne Rose

TITLE PAGE PHOTO
Steve and Dave Maslowski

BACK COVER PHOTOS
Left: Mary Lundeberg
Right: Snap Decision/Getty Images

*Cardinal,
page 150*

CHIEF CONTENT OFFICER
Jason Buhrmester

CONTENT DIRECTOR
Mark Hagen

CREATIVE DIRECTOR
Raeann Thompson

**ASSOCIATE CREATIVE
DIRECTOR** Kristen Stecklein

**MANAGER, PRODUCTION
DESIGN** Satyandra Raghav

**SENIOR PRINT PUBLICATION
DESIGNER** Sanjeev Dihman

DEPUTY EDITOR, COPY DESK
Ann M. Walter

COPY EDITOR Rayan Naqash

A *Birds & Blooms* Book

ISBN:
979-8-88977-055-8 (Hardcover)
979-8-88977-107-4 (Paperback)

Component Number:
118500124H

We are committed to both
the quality of our products
and the service we provide to
our customers. We value your
comments, so please feel free
to contact us at *TMBBookTeam@
TrustedMediaBrands.com.*

For more *Birds & Blooms* products
and information, visit our website:
www.birdsandblooms.com.

Hardcover printed in China
10 9 8 7 6 5 4 3 2 1

Paperback printed in China
10 9 8 7 6 5 4 3 2 1

Text, photography and illustrations
for *Beauty in the Backyard* are
based on articles previously
published in *Birds & Blooms*
magazine (*www.birdsandblooms
.com*).

Celebrate!

Relish nature's beauty all year long when you create a yard that truly celebrates all nature has to offer. From attracting favorite fliers in every season to landscaping with color and texture, the secrets to creating your own sanctuary are shared right here. You'll also find expert advice on house plants, front-porch decor and more. Open *Beauty in the Backyard* and revel in the easy ideas (and striking photos) sure to help you surround yourself in the seasonal backdrop of your dreams.

—THE EDITORS OF
BIRDS & BLOOMS MAGAZINE

CHAPTER 1

What a Colorful World

From the plumage of your favorite fliers to the brilliant blooms of garden greats, a bevy of colors is a sure way to lift spirits any time of year.

A Rainbow of Feathers

Five birds share the name grosbeak and sport similar thick bills—but the similarities stop there. Look for these colorful fliers throughout the U.S.

by Ken Keffer

NAMED FOR THEIR OVERSIZED BEAKS, grosbeaks use this handy utensil to crack tough seeds from the field edges of the Southeast to the boreal and montane forests of the North and West. Despite their similar beaks, grosbeak species aren't all related. Pine and evening grosbeaks are fancy finches, while rose-breasted, black-headed and blue grosbeaks are related to cardinals and buntings.

Ashley Peters, a professional working in conservation communications who has over a decade of experience bird-watching from Alaska to Louisiana, says grosbeaks are some of her favorites. "They are a bit out of the ordinary," she says.

Grosbeaks fill a variety of habitat niches, but most will visit feeders at least occasionally. "They are more special to see at feeders because you don't see them quite as often," Ashley says.

Male grosbeaks are among the most stunning birds out there. The females have a more subtle beauty. Grosbeaks, especially the females, can look quite similar to house, purple and Cassin's finches, but "the thicker, more substantial bills help give them away," Ashley says.

The best part is that these species are generally quite social, so you'll rarely see just a single bird.

Rose-breasted Grosbeak

Notable Field Marks: Males are nearly unmistakable, with snappy black-and-white patterns offset by bright red chests. Females and young birds look like oversized finches with a yellowish hue, fine streaks and a bold white eyebrow stripe.

Male rose-breasted grosbeak

Favorite Backyard Foods: Rose-breasted grosbeaks stop at hopper and tray feeders full of sunflower seeds during spring migration. They will also nibble at fruit and jelly.

Nesting Habits: Breeding from the Great Plains to the East Coast, they often select trees near forest edges or in more open, parklike woods.

Migration Notes: The spring arrival is much anticipated throughout the Midwest and eastern U.S. In the fall, look for them snacking on berries as they move south.

Fun Fact: The lovely song of the rose-breasted grosbeak is described as that of a robin who took singing lessons.

Black-headed Grosbeak

Notable Field Marks: Males are black and orange, while females and immature birds are fainter, showing more browns and a bit of streaking. Look for yellow underwings, which are visible in flight.

Favorite Backyard Foods: Black-headed grosbeaks eat seeds readily but they'll come to nectar and fruit feeders too. They also eat insects.

Nesting Habits: They often nest near streams and prefer mixed habitats with high plant diversity. The loose nature of the nests could aid in ventilation and keep eggs from overheating. Males help incubate eggs and raise the young.

Migration Notes: Black-headed grosbeaks are short-distance migrants, moving between southern Canada and the western United States to central Mexico.

Grosbeak Hybrids

Rose-breasted and black-headed grosbeak hybrids are a regular occurrence where their ranges overlap in the Great Plains, but in 2020, a one-of-a-kind rose-breasted grosbeak and scarlet tanager hybrid was documented in Pennsylvania.

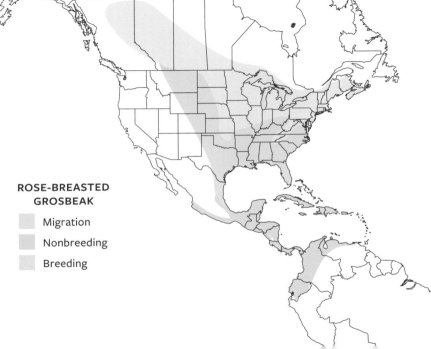

ROSE-BREASTED GROSBEAK

Migration

Nonbreeding

Breeding

Male (left) and female black-headed grosbeaks

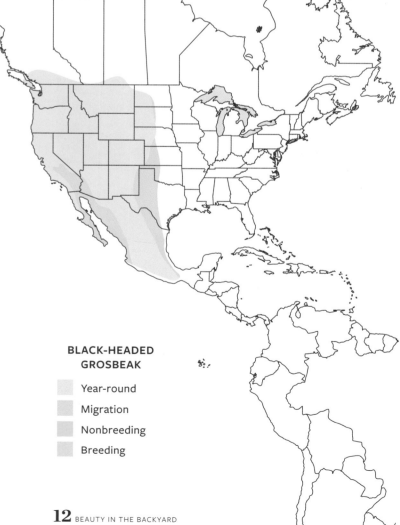

BLACK-HEADED GROSBEAK

Year-round

Migration

Nonbreeding

Breeding

Fun Fact: On their wintering grounds, black-headed grosbeaks are one of the few birds that can eat monarch butterflies, a species that is usually poisonous to predators.

Blue Grosbeak

Notable Field Marks: Cinnamon to chestnut brown wing bars are a feature for blue grosbeaks. Males are vibrant blue, while females and immature males have rich brown heads and show hints of blue along the backs, wings and tails. Watch for blue grosbeaks to twitch their tails sideways.

Favorite Backyard Foods: In addition to seeds, blue grosbeaks are not afraid of eating bigger bugs such as the praying mantis.

Nesting Habits: Blue grosbeaks are among the last species to return north and set up breeding territories. Look for them in shrubby areas or scrubby old fields and power line corridors.

Migration Notes: During fall migration, blue grosbeaks tend to fly straight south. In the West, they stick to overland routes arriving in Mexico, but eastern birds cross the Gulf of Mexico and island-hop to wintering grounds in the Caribbean.

Fun Fact: Blue grosbeaks are more closely related to lazuli buntings than they are to other grosbeaks.

Male blue grosbeak

Female blue grosbeak

BLUE GROSBEAK

Year-round

Migration

Nonbreeding

Breeding

Male evening grosbeak; female evening grosbeak (right)

EVENING GROSBEAK

	Year-round
	Year-round (scarce)
	Nonbreeding
	Nonbreeding (scarce)

Evening Grosbeak

Notable Field Marks: White wing patches are conspicuous on evening grosbeaks. Yellow is extensive in males but limited to the necks and flanks on females and immature birds.

Favorite Backyard Foods: They enjoy black oil sunflower seed, either in or out of the shell.

Nesting Habits: Historically a bird of the West, this grosbeak has a range that expanded beyond the Rockies in the mid-1800s. By the 1920s, they were regularly spotted in New England. In recent decades, eastern populations seem to be in decline.

Migration Notes: These grosbeaks are classic irruptive migrants, with great numbers moving far south every few years.

Fun Fact: Although evening grosbeaks make simple chirps and calls, the species doesn't use an elaborate song for establishing territories or attracting mates.

Pine Grosbeak

Notable Field Marks: Males are a different shade of red than a cardinal, more like a bigger version of a purple finch, according to Ashley. Females and immature males have gray bodies with orangish yellow heads, chests and rumps.

Favorite Backyard Foods: They are specialized to eat almost entirely tree buds, seeds and fruits, but they will eat sunflower seeds, suet and fruit on occasion.

Female pine grosbeak

Male pine grosbeak

PINE GROSBEAK

Year-round (scarce)

Nonbreeding (scarce)

Nesting Habits: Pine grosbeaks breed in evergreen forests across the boreal north and along the western mountains.

Migration Notes: Pine grosbeaks might show up in winter. The species is of one of the irruptive finch migrants, and flocks can show up nearly anywhere across the northern U.S.

Fun Fact: Pine grosbeaks are known for their somewhat tame nature and sluggish behavior.

Ideal Oriole Habitat

Plant shrubs, nectar plants and fruit-bearing trees to make your backyard more attractive to orioles. Try crabapple, raspberries, native honeysuckle and trumpet vine.

All About Oranges

Learn how to successfully attract orioles and other birds with sweet fruits

Nothin' Fancy

Perhaps one of the best things about oranges is their low maintenance. You don't need a snazzy feeder. Simply hammer a nail to a deck railing or fencepost and stick an orange half to the nail. Or set a couple of orange halves right in your platform feeder. Easy peasy!

Early Bird Gets the Orange

Try to anticipate when orioles will arrive in your backyard. You'll have the best chance of success if you put oranges out early. If orioles heading north find a good feeding spot, they may just stick around for breeding season and beyond, which means oriole guests for the entire summer.

Keep It Clean

As you can imagine, fresh fruit spoils quickly, especially in the spring and summer sunshine. Make sure to clean your fruit feeders every few days, remove moldy remains and replace with a fresh batch.

More Fruit Options

Don't stop at oranges. Birds who enjoy a sweet orange treat will often eat other ripe fruit too. Put out apple halves the same way as oranges. Set an overripe banana, a couple of handfuls of grapes or even chunks of melons on a platform feeder and have fun watching which birds fill up on fruit.

Reader Snapshot

As soon as I see the orioles come in, I put out oranges and grape jelly right away. (I don't like to put anything out too early.) Last year, the orioles stayed all summer and I was going through at least one or two oranges per day!

Rebecca Granger
BANCROFT, MI

Expert Advice

"If you're offering fruit for birds, you might just attract bonus winged visitors. Some butterflies and moths too are attracted to fruit!"

Kimberly Kaufman

B&B Tip

Orioles tend to steal the show in the backyard because of their bright colors, but other birds like oranges too. Look for these less showy birds that might stop for a citrusy snack:

- Gray catbirds
- Northern mockingbirds
- Red-bellied woodpeckers
- Western tanagers
- Brown thrashers
- Scarlet tanagers
- Rose-breasted grosbeaks

Now You See Them, Now You Don't

Many birds blend in with the background for their own survival—but you can spot them if you know how and where to look

by Ken Keffer

Black-and-white warbler

Eastern
screech-owl

Like chameleons matching their surroundings, ptarmigans molt with the seasons to evade predators.

White-tailed ptarmigan

Willow ptarmigan

Willow ptarmigan
in winter

BY NECESSITY, BIRDS ARE EXPERTS AT CAMOUFLAGE. There are clear exceptions, such as bright red male cardinals, but the rule is that birds thrive best when they're least noticeable. Nesting females are a good example: They are often dull in color so they blend in with their surroundings during the vulnerable nesting season. Another well-camouflaged bird is the goldfinch in winter; it molts into drab plumage so it's harder to see, even on bare branches.

But many birds are masters of disguise for all or most of the year, making them both a challenge and a thrill to discover. Here are a few cleverly masked birds you will want to watch out for, along with some tips on how to spot them.

Ptarmigan

One obvious benefit of camouflage is that it helps birds to hide from their enemies. Ptarmigan (including the willow, rock and white-tailed) are the champions of avian camouflage. Like chameleons matching their surroundings, ptarmigan molt with the seasons to evade predators. Mottled with warm browns during the summer and nearly completely white in the winter, ptarmigan change throughout the year. In the spring and fall, these chickenlike birds are dappled brown and white to mirror vegetation in transition.

TIP: One trick to spotting camouflaged birds is knowing their habitat. Look for ptarmigan walking low to the ground.

Great horned owl

Owls

Camouflage helps hide predators from potential prey, as well as from smaller birds that tend to harass these hunters. Most owls have heavy streaking and mottling to break up their silhouettes. At times it's nearly impossible to make out the shape of a great horned owl perched with its back against a tree trunk, or the outline of a snowy owl on the tundra. But the best camouflaged of these birds I've ever encountered was a screech-owl. I had found a small owl pellet, but I couldn't spot the bird for the life of me. Finally, some scolding chickadees alerted me to the owl's location: sitting in a clump of leaves, fully exposed on a slim branch.

TIP: For most owls, search the trees. Look for them close to the trunks; they usually don't venture very far out on the limbs.

American bittern

Harlequin duck

American Bittern

Heavily streaked plumage protects it well, but the American bittern has a trick that makes it even harder to spot in its marshy habitat. Bitterns will stick their bills up in the air to mimic surrounding reeds. They will even sway back and forth, doing a convincing cattail impression. I'd been staring right at a bittern and then suddenly lost sight of it. Bitterns move slowly and deliberately through the marsh, stalking fish, frogs and other small prey.

TIP: If you want to see bitterns, it's best to be patient and keep an eye out for even the smallest movement in a marsh.

Watch for Those Young 'uns

Juveniles are naturally vulnerable. Still learning how to fly and inexperienced at detecting predators, most birds wear drab plumage when they first fledge from the nest to increase their chance of survival. Some, such as robins, waxwings and even sparrows, also benefit from spots or streaks that help conceal their shape.

Ducks

The flamboyantly patterned harlequin duck seems as if it would stick out—until you try searching for one along the tumbling rapids of a stream where the birds nest. Female ducks of different species can pose tricky identification challenges, because they're so similarly patterned in brown scalloped feathers. While most males are dressed to impress during the breeding season, they too tend to molt into brown feathers for a period. Ducks are some of the only species that molt all their flight feathers at the same time. Being able to hide along the edges of lakes and ponds is especially critical, since they can't fly from danger for several weeks.

TIP: Want to spot a harlequin duck? Your best bet is to find one wintering along the northern ocean coasts or Great Lakes. Look for them standing along the rocky shores.

Creepers

Brown creepers have always looked to me like mice spiraling up the sides of tree trunks. They are similar to nuthatches but have gray-brown plumage that blends in perfectly with bark. Once I saw one napping on the side of a tree; the outline of the body was barely visible, but the posture of the bird caught my eye. Another fun fact: Creepers will sometimes tuck their nests behind sections of loose bark. A bird with similar habits is the black-and-white warbler, which can be just as difficult to spot against tree bark.

TIP: Creepers start low and work their way up a tree. So if you think you spot one, wait for it to fly, then follow it up the tree with your binoculars.

If you think you spot a creeper, wait for it to fly, then follow it with your binoculars

Brown creeper

Common nightjar

Nightjars

With their tapered bodies and oddly shaped heads, the nighthawks, whip-poor-wills and their relatives sometimes don't even look like birds to me. They'll perch and nest on the ground, on a tree branch, or sometimes even on the roof of a building. Even if you can spot their feathers, you may still have a hard time telling where the head is. Part of the reason is that nightjars have a cryptic pattern that breaks up their outline, allowing them to blend in with the background.

American woodcock

TIP: This is a tough one to offer a tip on. Keep your eyes on the ground, and make friends with local birders so they can help you find a nightjar when it's been sighted. There's strength in numbers!

Woodcocks

Although not related to nightjars, woodcocks are similar in many ways. They rely so heavily on remaining unseen that they will often sit tight rather than flying away, especially when incubating eggs. Like some of their shorebird relatives, woodcocks have long bills for probing. Sometimes they tuck their head down low, so the bill doesn't give them away as they wait for a potential predator to move along.

TIP: Find a woodcock walk in your area. Or go on your own during spring, right around dusk, when these birds perform their famous "dance" by suddenly zooming up into the air.

Sometimes birds make themselves highly visible—singing from the treetops, soaring through the sky or swimming gracefully. At other times, even the prettiest and most colorful birds can be difficult to see. The next time you have to do a double-take to spot one, take a moment to appreciate its natural camouflage in action.

Eastern kingbird

Counter-what?

The term is countershading. It refers to the coloration of birds with darker backs and lighter bellies, as in northern mockingbirds, eastern kingbirds and even shorebirds and gulls. This is another form of camouflage: From a distance, the dark back appears paler, while the paler belly appears darker, making the birds more difficult to spot.

Albinism in Birds

The answers behind the mysterious white-feathered bird in your backyard are revealed

by David Mizejewski

A tufted titmouse shows signs of albinism: pink legs and a pink bill.

O BSERVE BIRDS COMING AND GOING THROUGH A BACKYARD LONG ENOUGH, and eventually you'll spot one that has partially white or all-white feathers where there should be color. These birds have a genetic condition known as leucism or, more rarely, albinism, which affects their coloring as well as their ability to survive in the wild. The next time you spot one of these fascinating birds, you'll know if it's leucistic or albino.

Albinism

Birds that lack the color pigment melanin have a genetic mutation called albinism. These birds are often pure white, but in some cases an albino bird might still have yellow or orange feathers. Those warmer colors are carotenoid pigments, rather than melanin ones, so they're still present in birds with albinism. The true test of whether a bird is an albino is in its eyes. The lack of melanin allows blood vessels to show through, causing their eyes to be bright pink or red.

On the other end of the color spectrum is a genetic condition called melanism, in which a bird has extra melanin pigmentation. These birds appear darker than the typical coloration for their species.

Leucism

Often confused with albinism is a lesser-known genetic condition called leucism, in which not just melanin but other color pigments are reduced as well. Unlike albinism, leucism doesn't completely

Despite her lack of blue coloring, this female eastern bluebird found a mate.

eliminate pigment. Leucistic birds appear lighter than normal but aren't fully white. Sometimes these birds are pale, with an overall lightening of their coloring. In other cases, leucism can result in a bird being pied or piebald—with white patches across its body. Because they don't fully lack melanin, leucistic birds have normal-colored eyes rather than the pink or red eyes of albinos.

Albinism Impact

Compared to typically colored members of their species, albino birds are at a great disadvantage. The white feathers stand out against vegetation; thus, without camouflage, albino birds are easier for predators to spot. Their feathers offer some protection in snow, but unfortunately they reduce a bird's ability to retain heat. Dark colors absorb heat, light colors reflect it, which can mean life or death in freezing temperatures.

Birds with albinism suffer from weak feathers due to a lack of melanin. Their feathers break and deteriorate over time. Albino birds also have poor eyesight—another hindrance. As a result, these birds rarely survive past fledging.

Leucistic birds have slightly better chances because they retain some pigmentation. That means the light-colored bird you see in your yard is more likely leucistic than albino.

Either way, it's a rare and exciting sight when such a unique bird stops for a visit!

The white patches covering this American robin are a hint that it is leucistic, not albino.

Five Facts About Discoloration

- Genetics determine true albino birds: Both parents have to carry the uncommon recessive genes that produce rare pure-white offspring.

- A pied or piebald bird's leucistic feathers are rarely in a symmetrical pattern.

- Typically, leucism affects only dark feathers, so some birds with leucism have white feathers while still maintaining the bright colors of their red, orange or yellow feathers.

- A bird is a true albino if its feet, legs, bill and eyes are pale pink or red.

- Birds with discoloration may struggle during courtship. Many birds use plumage color as a way to find and recognize potential mates.

Q What's going on with this beautiful bird?

Fae Montgomery
CONKLIN, MI

Kenn and Kimberly: When birds have unusual conditions affecting their pigment, they can show one-of-a-kind coloration. This bird appears to be an American goldfinch lacking melanin in its feathers, a condition called leucism. Melanin creates brown, black or gray coloring. Since this finch is in its winter plumage, most of its body would normally be brown, with black in the wings and tail—but those colors have been replaced by white. The wash of yellow around the head, produced by a different kind of pigment, is still present.

Q Is this hairy woodpecker immature, or does it just have unusual coloration?

Audrey Mihalko
BOONVILLE, NY

Kenn and Kimberly: That's an interesting-looking bird! Immature hairy woodpeckers can show some brown in their feathers, but we don't think this is a very young bird because it doesn't have the loose and fluffy feathers of a fledgling. The feathers with brown on them appear to be fairly fresh, so we think the color is a result of unusual pigment, not anything related to the bird's age.

Q I took this photo at our bird feeder last October. Could this bird be a cross between a snow bunting and a redpoll?

Ken Thommes HILLMAN, MN

Kenn and Kimberly: This bird does suggest both a snow bunting and redpoll, but we believe it's a purple finch with leucistic plumage, lacking dark pigments from some of the feathers. The bird is shaped like a purple finch, with a thick bill, long wingtips and a notched tail tip. The normal dark brown color shows on the tail and many wing feathers, and it looks red and pink in many of the same areas where you'd see those colors on an adult male purple finch. This leucistic bird is one of a kind!

Two years ago, I noticed a male northern cardinal frequenting my double cherry tree every morning. My goal was to get a picture of him, surrounded by the pink cherry blossoms while they were still in bloom. After a couple weeks of waiting, I finally got the picture I wanted.

Alan Haailston VIRGINIA BEACH, VA

This photo represents a first for me—I had never seen a red-headed woodpecker in my backyard before. It stayed on the suet feeder for quite some time, giving me plenty of opportunity to admire its brilliant colors.

Catherine M. Smith
ISLIP, NY

I just put my oriole feeder outside when this Baltimore oriole stopped by for a picture. I love the contrast of the red begonia with the orange breast of the oriole.

Craig Watts
HARTSBURG, MO

Don't you love it when you're in the right place at the right time? In late May, I was in the kitchen making hummingbird nectar and happened to glance out the window. A male western tanager was sitting on my oriole feeder, which I'd filled with orange marmalade. A tiny drip on his beak revealed he'd already had a taste. I snapped several photos before this brilliant creature flew away.

GeriAnne Abeyta
ESPANOLA, NM

My attempts to master organic gardening were falling short, and I was almost ready to give up on the endeavor entirely. Then, one afternoon, the sun seemed to rise from the center of my garden as buttery yellow goldfinches took flight. When I hadn't been looking, my fledgling organic garden had grown a beautiful bouquet.

Jane High
NASHVILLE, TN

My husband, Steve, and I were very fortunate to have a female ruby-throated hummingbird regularly visit our flowers and sugar-water feeder one summer. By the end of June, three ruby-throats started showing up. We are almost certain this ruby-throated hummingbird is one of the fledglings.

Janice Neitzel GULF SHORES, AL

During the winter months here in Florida, I like to visit J.N. "Ding" Darling National Wildlife Refuge in Sanibel. When the tide goes out, many bird species flock to the refuge to feed. I photographed a snowy egret as it searched for food on a sandbar.

Donna Chesney NAPLES, FL

A nice breeze was blowing through the window, and I was focused on a great blue heron, when I heard a very loud bird. I looked over and spotted the most colorful boat-tailed grackle begging for my attention. I was pleasantly surprised by the colors and how calm the bird was while I excitedly snapped multiple photos.

Kerri McMullen
INDIAN HARBOUR BEACH, FL

I took this photo of a common loon on her nest. Loons are difficult to get close to and most people (myself included) assume it is just a black and white bird, but there is a beautiful iridescent turquoise patch at the base of her neck in addition to the intricate black and white plumage.

Bill Dinkins
MAINEVILLE, OH

Fall Foliage Secrets

Experts share why leaves change—and predict when to hit the road for the colorful show

by Sheryl DeVore

Autumn leaves in hues of orange, yellow and red dot the trees at Great Smoky Mountains National Park.

KATHY MATHEWS LOVES TO WATCH THE SUGAR MAPLES turn yellow, orange and red at Great Smoky Mountains National Park near her home. "Sometimes you'll see all three colors on the same leaf," she says.

An associate professor of biology at Western Carolina University, Kathy has spent 10 years studying and predicting peak viewing time for fall colors. She still marvels at the magic of fall, when green leaves transform into copper shades.

This phenomenon occurs when trees stop producing chlorophyll, a green substance in leaves that interacts with sunlight throughout spring and summer to make food for trees to grow. Changing weather conditions in fall tell the trees it's time to store sugars in the roots for next year's growth. As the cool temperatures approach, daylight hours shorten and the chlorophyll breaks down, revealing the bright hidden hues.

"It is more efficient for the tree to do this than to maintain its leaves year-round," Kathy says. Some trees, including maples, even create a new pigment—a deep rich red.

A dappled sassafras leaf rests on the dark ground

A cute tufted titmouse amid a sweetgum tree's bright fall leaves

Weather conditions in the spring, summer and fall affect the timing and the brightness of autumn leaves. A dry summer may mean more vibrant colors, Kathy says, "although that's not good for the overall health of the tree." On the other hand, a rainy summer results in duller hues. And a sunny, dry fall produces more of the deep red pigments.

"For the best fall color, you want a gradual but steady temperature change," Kathy says. "You want the nighttime temperature to continue to dip to freezing to make all of the trees come into full color at once."

And that's when the magic happens. This annual spectacle occurs all over the country, so you can enjoy it in your town or even your own backyard. Many folks, however, prefer to catch the show on the road. When planning an autumn color viewing vacation, it's best to set aside several days to a week.

Kathy recommends checking the time of the average annual first frost at your destination. "Plan your vacation for a couple of weeks after the first frost, to hit color

Color Your World

Make the magic happen in your own backyard with these trees and shrubs.

Aspen: yellow

Bald cypress: orange, red

Beech: golden yellow to bronze

Black tupelo: yellow, orange, scarlet, purple

Red maple: red

Sassafras: yellow, orange, scarlet, purple

Shagbark hickory: golden yellow

Sourwood: yellow, purple, red

Sugar maple: red, yellow, orange

Sweetgum: yellow, purple, red

at its peak," she says. "A freezing temperature is what starts the breakdown of chlorophyll. You can predict leaves will start changing about three or four days after the first frost." She also suggests visiting websites for the places you want to go to learn more about typical fall color patterns.

Cruise 70-mile Million Dollar Highway through Colorado to see epic fall color.

Because of the unpredictability, visit an area with various elevations for the best chance of viewing many colors across the landscape in one day, says Paul Super, science coordinator at the Great Smoky Mountains National Park.

"In the Smokies and other mountainous areas, the peak time for color changes with elevation," he says. "You can come over a wide range of days, and the fall colors pass peak at high elevations earlier than the low elevations." High spots in the Smokies, with a climate similar to New England, see yellow birch turn bright yellow amid the reds of mountain ashes, sometimes as early as mid-September.

At lower elevations, you can observe peak colors of sugar maples, hickories, sweetgums and other trees from early to mid-October through early November.

Paul suggests not overlooking oak trees, which are among the last to change colors. They produce russet, red and yellow-brown leaves, depending on weather conditions.

No matter where you are in fall, remember that the natural world is constantly changing. "You have to take your chances on when the best colors will arrive," Paul says. "But you'll always find something beautiful."

Franconia Notch State Park in New Hampshire comes alive with coppery hues.

Fall Foliage Hot Spots
Visit these colorful locales for a front-row seat at the show.

New York
Mountain Clove Run, Catskill Mountains September through early October

Michigan
Keweenaw Peninsula Late September, early October

Colorado
Aspen Late September, mid-October

New Mexico
Enchanted Circle Scenic Byway Late September, early October

New Hampshire
Kancamagus Highway Early October

Tennessee, North Carolina
Blue Ridge Parkway, Great Smoky Mountains National Park October

Wisconsin
County Road 42, Door County Mid-October

Massachusetts
Mohawk Trail Mid-October

Georgia
Russell-Brasstown Scenic Byway, Blue Ridge Mountains Mid- to late October

Oregon
Colombia River Gorge Late October

(Peak foliage times are approximate)

Evergreen Gardens

Classic conifers add timeless appeal to landscapes. Choose the perfect type for your yard and learn how to keep it healthy.

by Luke Miller

Mix species of evergreens with different textures and colors to create a visually appealing landscape.

Cape May warbler on a spruce

Create a lush look by adding a mix of conifers, including dwarf Alberta spruce, near the borders of plots.

GARDENERS LOVE EVERGREEN
TREES—especially in winter when
these enduring plants offer the only
living color we're likely to see in the
landscape. But the backyard classics
offer benefits beyond the chilliest season: They
can screen out ugly elements, lend privacy,
provide a backdrop for other plants and block
strong winds.

"A screen of evergreen trees can be utilized
to provide a windbreak around homes, which
can reduce both winter heating and summer
cooling costs," says Paul Tauke, forester for the
city of Ames, Iowa, and former chief of the Iowa
Department of Natural Resources' Forestry
Bureau. "Placing evergreens on the north
and west sides of the property provides the
most effective wind protection."

Evergreens aren't just loved by humans—
backyard visitors adore them too.

"The primary wildlife benefits of evergreens
are winter protection and nesting habitat," Paul
says. He notes that spruces and pines provide
excellent cover for birds and that evergreens
with edible cones, such as eastern red cedars, are
a valuable food source, especially to waxwings.
Just consider what could be invasive in your
region. Paul points out that an eastern red
cedar's seeds are spread through birds and are
often considered invasive in prairie, grassland
and pasture situations.

Choose Your Greenery

Although a couple of evergreens are broadleaf
(meaning their foliage looks more like a
traditional leaf), needled conifers, including
pine, spruce and fir, have more value to wildlife.
Paul's favorites are white spruce, Norway spruce,
concolor fir, white pine, Leyland cypress and
arborvitae, but he says to avoid planting Austrian
or Scotch pine, both of which can have serious
diseases.

Kirtland's warblers, like this adult, nest exclusively in jack pines.

Black Hills spruce

American arborvitae

Species for Tough Spots

The University of Minnesota Extension suggests these evergreens for difficult conditions.

Clay soil: arborvitae, ponderosa pine, white fir

Sandy soil: mugo pine, many junipers

Wet soil: American arborvitae, balsam fir, black spruce

High PH: arborvitae, Black Hills spruce, mugo pine, ponderosa pine

Windy Areas: jack pine, red pine, ponderosa pine, Rocky Mountain juniper, savin juniper, Douglas fir

Partial sun: arborvitae, balsam fir, Douglas fir

Shade: Canada hemlock, Canada yew, Japanese yew

White fir

Gold Cone juniper

Canada hemlock

Blueberry Delight juniper

Anna's Magic Ball arborvitae

Mugo pine

"Because of diseases like cytospora canker and rhizosphaera needle cast, Colorado blue spruce should also be avoided in windbreaks and in any other areas where airflow through the tree is restricted by structures or other trees," Paul says. There are great evergreens for many different conditions and spaces. As a bonus, many standard-sized species are now available in space-saving dwarf or columnar form.

Plant Smart

After you choose a tree or shrub, pay attention to where you plan to grow it.

"As a general rule, evergreens do not tolerate wet feet, so place them in areas where the soil has good drainage," Paul says. "Be aware that many residential urban sites may have had the topsoil removed in the land development process. If this is the case, any tree that's planted could be put in clay soil. Clay soils are typically poorly draining, so evergreens may find it difficult to thrive."

Here's another option that's more moisture-proof: bald cypress. It's a deciduous conifer that masquerades as an evergreen until fall, when it changes color and drops its needles.

When planting any conifer, dig a hole just as deep as the root ball (so the root flair is even with the soil surface), but twice as wide. Then backfill with the excavated soil, not amended soil. "Research shows that adding gravel, sand or black dirt in the planting hole does not improve drainage and is actually detrimental to the tree," Paul says.

Skyhigh WB Norway spruce (above) is a miniature shrub. Its dense green foliage grows only 1 foot high.

Water Well

Unlike deciduous trees, there's rarely a need to rake around the base of the tree or to prune evergreens—instead, focus on water.

"Evergreens typically need more supplemental watering than deciduous trees in the first few years following planting, especially if the weather turns hot and dry," says Paul. Look at the diameter of the tree trunk to know how much water you need—use 10 gallons for every inch.

But be cautious of overwatering. Stick your finger a few inches into the ground to feel if the soil is crumbly. If it's dry, then it's time to water.

Take Care

After planting, evergreens are generally easy to maintain. Just remember two things: Mulch and do not fertilize.

Mulching conserves moisture and keeps roots cool. Leave a saucer-sized space near the base of the tree clear of mulch. This keeps material away from the trunk, protecting the base of the tree from pests and disease.

There's no need to fertilize newly planted evergreens. "Most fertilizers contain nitrogen and that stimulates leaf or needle growth," Paul says. "Typically, newly planted trees need to reestablish roots that were lost in the transplanting process, so using nitrogen in the first two or three years after planting can stimulate top growth before an adequate root system has developed. This could lead to the tree drying out if weather turns hot and dry."

If you follow these tips, your trees and shrubs will surely reward you—and the wild birds—for years to come.

Gardening with Color

Plant the right hues to create a warm and inviting backyard space

by Tammi Hartung

Bright orange crocosmia and beautiful pink hydrangeas add zest to both sides of this garden bridge.

GARDENS ARE THE ESSENCE OF COLOR. Visitors will experience a garden differently depending on what color scheme the flowers and foliage create. They may find it tranquil or invigorating, simply because of how the garden's colors work together. Wildlife visitors are drawn to color too. With the right hues, you can invite birds, butterflies and more to your backyard. Ready for your lesson in color? Let's begin!

Embrace the Classics

Blues, purples and pinks are favorites for gardeners. For some beautiful purple and blue flower options, look to lavender, campanulas, salvia and lupines. Equally nice are pink blooms like purple coneflowers, cosmos and hollyhocks. Don't overdo it, though. Flowers in the purple, pink and blue color range give the garden a lovely watercolor look, which can have a very peaceful and relaxing effect on visitors strolling along the garden path. However, stand back 10 feet or more from the garden, and it's a completely different effect. The colors tend to blend together so well that the garden loses much of its definition. Onlookers will see only a bluish or pinkish blur.

Add Contrast

To break up your pink and purple garden, you'll want to look to the next color grouping—oranges, reds and yellows. These shades create an atmosphere that is invigorating, uplifting and feisty! Choosing plants like black-eyed Susans, poppies, zinnias and Mexican sunflowers will make you feel happy and energized in no time.

Many of those warm-colored flowers will also welcome pollinators and birds to the garden. For example, butterflies can't resist the bright blooms of sunflowers and butterfly weed. Nearly every red tubular flower, such as penstemon or salvia, will attract hummingbirds, and Mexican sunflower seeds are irresistible to goldfinches and other seed eaters.

Cosmos

The No-Color Rule

You might not think of white flowers as a colorful garden staple but they are. Including enough white flowering plants and those with silver-gray foliage is an important aspect in planning any garden. Strive for a garden that has 30% of its plants fall in this category.

White flowers or silver-gray foliage brighten up the garden, giving it a fresh look. This is especially important in the heat of summer or at the end of the season when the garden begins to take on a tired look. If you have some white baby's breath or chamomile planted throughout the garden, their white blooms will add a cheerful touch. The same thing happens when woolly lamb's ears, Greek mullein and gray santolina are thrown in the mix, because all of them have silver-gray foliage.

Along with other colors, white flowers also attract plenty of beneficial insects. Ladybugs, lacewings, and hoverflies hunt pests like aphids and are just a few of the helpful insects you can expect to find in your garden. Having abundance of these insects in the garden translates to a garden mostly free of pests, so you don't need pesticides.

Don't Forget Foliage

Finally, embrace color and texture in any garden by taking advantage of different types of foliage. There are many interesting shades of green and gold foliage, as well as purple and red in plants such as red rubin basil or shiso. The endless

Top Picks for Color

Flowers of purple and blue

1. Catmint 2. Rosemary 3. Verbena

Flowers of pink

4. Hollyhock 5. Yarrow 6. Rhododendron

Flowers of yellow

7. Black-eyed Susan 8. Goldenrod 9. Rue

varieties of shapes and textures of the leaves will keep any garden visitor interested in the landscape.

Mugwort, although invasive in some areas, is a great perennial with red stems and deeply cut leaves, which are green on top and silvery underneath. When a breeze comes, this plant shimmers. Bronze fennel, with bronzy green foliage and yellow flowers, is a tall plant that makes an attractive statement wherever it grows. There's the fine foliage of fountain grass and the leathery feel to tulip or iris leaves. All of these plants create interest, complement flowers and make the garden a true place of beauty.

Variegated foliage is nearly a whole garden world by itself, with many variegated thymes, dianthus, oreganos and more. Use a bit of care with some golden variegations in foliage, though, because they sometimes clash if planted next to chartreuse or bright pink flowers. Intermixing variegated foliage with rich solid leaf colors of any shade will make your garden look stunning.

More Picks for Color

Flowers of orange and red

1. Butterfly weed 2. Calendula 3. Jupiter's beard

Flowers of white

4. Phlox 5. Alyssum 6. Shasta daisy

Foliage of silver and gray

7. Helichrysum 8. Gray santolina 9. Woolly lamb's ears

Little Black Plant

The hot new color is black in the world of horticulture. Check out some of our favorites.

by Stacy Tornio

WHEN I FIRST heard about black plants, I didn't understand what the fuss was all about. Plants and flowers are supposed to be bright and colorful. Why would anyone want dark and dreary?

But then I saw my first black petunia—wow! I couldn't believe how gorgeous and captivating it was. My newfound love didn't stop with petunias. Once I started looking, I began noticing all kinds of cool plants with dark, rich foliage and blooms. While some were really more like black wannabes, falling into the purple or brown section of the color wheel, I was still impressed with the selection. Take a look at some of my favorites, but be sure to do a little exploring on your own as well. After all, I hear every garden looks good in black.

‹ Zwartkop aeonium

(*AEONIUM ARBOREUM*, ZONES 9 TO 11)

It's hard to find a more dramatic and impressive black plant than this black rose aeonium. This succulent does best in at least a half day of full sun. If grown in more shade, the rosettes are reddish-purple with a green center. It grows up to 12 inches tall and tolerates drought and poor soil. If you live out of Zone 9 to 11 (and let's face it, you probably do), then overwinter it indoors!

Why we love it: Though it looks stunning with some bright yellow petunias or pansies, we think it makes a statement all on its own.

⌃ Midnight Ruffles hellebore

(*HELLEBORUS*, ZONES 4-9)

This double-bloom hellebore actually has three times as many petals as a single-bloom hellebore. Combine that with its amazing velvety flowers, and it's easy to see why this plant has the horticulture world talking. It grows nearly 24 inches tall and wide, and is ideal for shade.

Why we love it: It's an early bloomer! Hellebores start flowering in late winter and continue for several weeks. In fact, it's also known as Lenten rose, because some varieties bloom during Lent.

⌃ Tropicanna Black canna

(*CANNA*, ZONES 7 TO 11)

Boasting bright scarlet blooms, the Tropicanna Black series offers a refreshing alternative for cannas. You'll need to plant the rhizomes every spring. Then sit back and watch the magic as they grow up to 6 feet tall. The plants do best with at least six hours of sun, but will tolerate some shade.

Why we love it: It's one of the easiest ways to bring the flair of the tropics to your backyard.

‹ Black Velvet petunia

(*PETUNIA X HYBRID*, ANNUAL)

Are you ready for the world's first black petunia? Here it is! Ball Horticulture Co. introduced Black Velvet a few years ago. A perfect fit for containers, it thrives in sunny areas.

Why we love it: Containers just got more interesting, thanks to the richness of this plant. Pair it with bright-pink blooms for a lively contrast.

⌃ Sorbet Black Delight viola

(*VIOLA CORNUTA*, ANNUAL)

Also known as horned violet, this low-maintenance, fragrant viola tolerates sun and partial shade and blooms most profusely in cool weather. Everyone should grow some violas, so why not try this bold cultivar?

Why we love it: You know how you get that itch to garden even before the chance of frost has passed? Grow this—it's forgiving.

❯ Black Prince coleus

(*COLEUS SOLENOSTEMON*, ANNUAL)

You'll have plenty of versatility with this tough coleus—it does well in sun or shade and is perfect for container combinations, hanging baskets or garden beds. (You can even grow it as a houseplant.) It grows to about 30 inches tall and will attract hummingbirds with its late-season flowers.

Why we love it: It's very forgiving if you sometimes forget to water it. If you see it start to droop, just add water and it'll perk right up.

⌃ Black Coral elephant ear

(*COLOCASIA ESCULENTA*, ZONES 7-10)

Elephant ear is a plant that already commands attention with its giant leaves. This black-leafed variety is even more striking, growing nearly 4 feet tall with leaves 3 feet or more across! Even if you live in a colder zone, you can enjoy this beauty year after year. Just dig it up and keep it in a cool place over winter.

Why we love it: It's one of the most distinctive plants for containers, but you're going to need a big one! Plant it as the centerpiece and accent with bright plants around it.

⌃ Victoriana Silver Lace Black primrose
(*PRIMULA ELATIOR*, ZONES 5 TO 10)

As winter turns to spring, little blooms appear on these compact dark-green plants. Victoriana Silver Lace Black boasts white-edged petals and a golden yellow center. The primrose does best in partial shade, but it can live in full sun if the soil around it remains moist.

Why we love it: The pattern! The standout colors remind us of a kaleidoscope.

⌃ Before the Storm tall bearded iris
(*IRIS*, ZONES 3-10)

Irises are a staple in backyard gardens, and they're available in just about every shade imaginable, including this new purplish black variety. This one has a bit of a sweet fragrance and blooms in early summer, making it the perfect plant to provide garden color in the lull between tulips and flowering perennials. Like all tall bearded irises, it performs best in full sun.

Why we love it: It's naturally deer- and rabbit-resistant, so if you have trouble with critters eating your plants, give it a try.

❮ Obsidian coral bells
(*HEUCHERA*, ZONES 3 TO 9)

While coral bells do have tiny blooms atop long shoots, many people buy them for the foliage. And why wouldn't you, with options like deep red, orange and black. This Obsidian cultivar is just one of several coral bells with black leaves.

Why we love it: You can plant coral bells in partial shade. And the tiny blooms attract hummingbirds!

Q I bought a croton several years ago because I liked the different colors in the leaves. Now my plant is doing well, but it generates big green leaves. Why aren't they colorful?

Larry Smith
HUDSON, NH

Melinda: Crotons display the best leaf color when grown outdoors or in a sunny window indoors. All plants contain three pigments—chlorophyll (green), carotinoids (yellow and yellow-oranges) and anthocyanins (red and purple). The carotinoids and anthocyanins mask some or all of the green cholorphyll in plants with colorful leaves. In low light conditions, the green chlorophyll pigment becomes more pronounced than the other two pigments. Move your plant to a sunnier window and you should see an improvement in the leaf color.

Q Pink moss roses have come up every year in our flower bed for the past 15 years. This is the first time we've ever seen a white flower produced. What are the chances it will continue to come up as a white bloom in the future?

Deborah Whiting MIDLAND, TX

Melinda: Moss roses are self-seeding annuals that can return to the same general location for many years. Hybrid cultivars do not always produce duplicate offspring. Cross-pollination and mutations also result in changes in flower color, plant size and growth habit. The white flowers may continue to appear and produce additional white offspring, or this may have been a one-time occurrence. Enjoy the surprise!

Q The leaves on our Japanese maple usually turn red before dropping. But last year the leaves turned beige and stayed on the tree all winter. What happened?

Sherry Lesiak POWELL, OH

Melinda: Blame it on the weather. A sudden drop in temperature can prevent the normal process of leaves turning color in autumn and then falling from the tree. Gradual cooling allows the trees to form a barrier, called the abscission layer, between the leaves and twigs, which helps the leaves detach. When we have a warmer than normal fall followed by a sudden or extreme drop in temperature, plants can't always completely form the abscission layer. The leaves eventually turn brown and remain on the tree.

CHAPTER 2

Take It Inside

Bring nature's beauty indoors with houseplants, flower arrangements, terrariums and other ideas found in this handy chapter.

The Art of Houseplants

10 tips from a designer about styling your indoor green spaces

by Melissa Lo

THE PRINCIPLES OF DESIGN ARE RULES that designers use in combination to create a visual that is effective and aesthetically pleasing. Typically used in the art and design world, these principles and their relationship with each other work together to create a sense of harmony and cohesiveness.

As a designer, I practice and apply these principles when styling plants in the home. I've found so much joy in being inspired by nature and injecting elements of the earth and bringing them right into my living spaces. These principles have become an everyday part of life and have developed and shaped my personal style and taste as I continue to transform every nook into a relaxing green retreat.

Use one, several or as many principles as you see fit, keeping the rules in mind when shopping for plants or as you are styling the home. Below are my top design principles for styling your green spaces.

1. Think about hierarchy.

Also known as emphasis or focal point, hierarchy implies importance in a visual arrangement. When combining plants in a group, rank each by its characteristic feature in descending order, with your focal point having the highest ranking. Hierarchy can be reinforced through contrast in proximity, size, color, texture and shape.

Hierarchy

PHOTO AND ILLUSTRATIONS: MELISSA LO

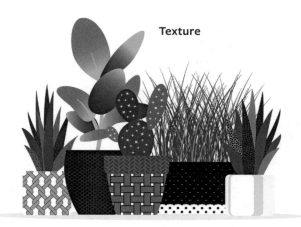

Texture

2. Choose plants and pots with various textures.

Texture describes the surface quality by appearance, feel or consistency of an element or object. Bring compositions to life and put them in context by introducing or highlighting textures with plants and surrounding decor. Textures can be found on the leaves and other parts of a plant, created by the plant as a whole along with the container it is placed into.

Shape

3. Have fun with shapes.

Shape is defined by the form or outline of an element. For houseplants, this could be the shape of a leaf combined with other parts of the plant or an entire silhouette of a specimen, including the container it is housed in. The irregular lines of plants can help soften a look and give an organic feel to a space. Enhance these natural curves by introducing natural fiber, wooden and stone elements into spaces.

4. Employ white space wisely.

White space consists of the areas of a visual that do not contain any elements. These are the areas that are essentially empty, which can help to frame and highlight a group of plants or a vignette by increasing visibility and emphasis.

White Space

5. Create contrast.

Contrast refers to the juxtaposition between two opposing elements. These differences or opposites help create interest, impact and emphasis in a visual. Contrast in plants can be achieved by juxtaposition in color, texture, shape, size or the containers they are housed in.

Contrast

6. Rely on repetition.

Also known as rhythm or similarity, repetition uses the same or similar elements in design. Using this principle helps to create unity, consistency and cohesiveness. Repetition is not only limited to the use of the same or similar plants, but can also be applied to the planters they are housed in.

Repetition

Variety

9. Place plants in groups.

The relationship between objects can be emphasized when they are placed in a group, allowing the viewer to draw connections between similar elements. Grouping related varieties of plants from the same genus, by growth habits or even a combination of similar planters—cactuses in cement planters, ferns in a collection of glass terrariums, pothos in matte black planters—are examples of creating visually cohesive results.

Grouping

7. Mix it up.

Adding contrasting elements can help diversify and create visual interest. Combine different species of plants with varying colors, sizes, shapes and textures to create the complexity and dynamics to achieve variety. This can also be achieved with the addition of inanimate objects such as artwork, keepsakes, souvenirs or other items of personal interest.

10. Lead the eye.

Movement describes the path that is created to help the viewer's eye scan from one element to the next. This can be achieved by the direction created through lines, shapes, colors and edges of plants and the containers they are put in. As an example, create movement by staggering trailing plants on a shelf to lead the eye from the top left corner to the bottom right, as we are naturally trained to read a page.

8. Keep it simple.

The principle of simplicity is the discipline of reducing, refining and editing a design to create the most impact. Sometimes less is more. Try removing one, two or even a few elements and take a step back to see how it affects the overall composition of your design.

Reprinted with permission from *Houseplant Oasis* by Melissa Lo. Page Street Publishing Co. 2022.

Movement

Q Do you have any hacks to keep houseplants perfectly watered?

Hannah Smith PORTLAND, OR

Melinda: Gardeners can extend the time between watering with a few gadgets. Plant nannies, glass watering bulbs and similar items hold and distribute water over time. You can also amend the soil with organic products such as wool pellets. The pellets hold more water than soil and reduce the need for water by up to 25%. Just incorporate this product into the potting mix when planting or repotting. Another option is self-watering pots. Keep the reservoir filled, and water is released into the houseplant's soil as needed. You'll be watering much less often with these containers.

What's your best houseplant hack?

Readers share their top tips for growing healthy indoor plants

I placed a long **sofa table so that half of it is in front of a south-facing window**. Plants that prefer a lot of light are in the area in front of the window. But because the other half of the table is in the shade, I can have many plants in one spot, and they are all happy.

Hope Cate WILMINGTON, NC

Add coffee grounds to your houseplants and watch them thrive.

Delores Koland PELICAN RAPIDS, MN

Use a soil moisture meter to prevent overwatering. It lets you know if the soil is wet, moist or dry.

Tracy McCullum JOLIET, IL

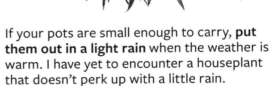

If your pots are small enough to carry, **put them out in a light rain** when the weather is warm. I have yet to encounter a houseplant that doesn't perk up with a little rain.

Robbin Moller SYLVANIA, OH

I put ice cubes in my hanging plants. As the ice melts, the soil absorbs the water and it doesn't drip out the bottom of the pot.

Roslyn Francis LODI, CA

Give the plants a quarter-turn once a week to even out their exposure to the sun.

Judy Roberts GRAYTOWN, OH

Houseplants for a Healthy Home

Surround yourself with greenery to make a good-for-you difference. Here's what experts say about the mental boost and their top plant picks.

by Lauren David

RESEARCH SHOWS THAT BEING IN THE presence of nature has many benefits, whether you're walking in a forest, working in a small garden or keeping a few household plants.

"One study showed that patients at a hospital who had plants in their rooms reported less pain, lower blood pressure, less fatigue and less anxiety than patients without plants in their rooms," says Jenny Seham, attending psychologist and assistant clinical professor at the Albert Einstein College of Medicine in New York City.

She says that this has a good explanation: "Cortisol, the stress hormone, has been shown to lower with plant interaction, lowering fatigue, irritability and blood pressure." She adds that gardening and caring for plants can help people turn away from negative thoughts and emotions.

Gayle Weill, a licensed clinical social worker in New York, Connecticut and Florida, says raising plants is an opportunity to practice true presence in the here and now. "Rather than dwelling on the past or worrying about the future, plant care helps one focus on the present moment and provides a feeling of accomplishment," she says.

Check out these eight top plant suggestions to brighten your home and improve your mental health.

SPIDER PLANT

This plant is both pretty and useful. Spider plants can help remove formaldehyde and carbon monoxide from the air.

Pothos

Pothos are adaptable plants with waxy green, chartreuse or even variegated heart-shaped leaves.

"They can exist in a lot of different ways, as they grow long vines that can trail or hang from a pot and grow downward," says Tyler Keith, a licensed clinical social worker in North Carolina and an avid gardener. As a bonus, pothos also looks fantastic when supported with a trellis.

Aloe Vera

Aloe vera is a novice plant owner's dream, because it's forgivable, adaptable and helpful to have around the house. Seham says, "Aloe vera produces a healing gel that you can use straight from the leaf."

"I recommend having an aloe in the home, as it is helpful for burns, cuts and scrapes," says Keith. The juice from the leaves soothes pain, he adds, and helps injuries heal faster. That goes for sunburn too.

Lavender

A beautiful herb that attracts plenty of pollinators, lavender is also well known for its relaxing scent. It "has a calming effect, aids in reducing stress, promotes sleep and has anti-inflammatory properties when used as a topical for skin," Weill says.

This means it's great both in the garden and indoors, if you have a very sunny spot. Be sure to keep it in a pot near a window with lots of light if you grow it inside. Some gardeners need artificial growing lights to keep their plants happy. You can clip and dry the sprigs, and then keep them in a bowl inside your home or even sprinkle them in your bathtub.

Snake Plant

Sword-shaped with dark green leaves, the snake plant's mustard yellow or white stripes make it stand out. Plus, it's ideal for newer plant parents.

"Snake plants are patient with new gardeners, as they are not quick to cook in the sun and die. These plants are great for building your confidence in your plant-care skills," says Keith.

Pothos

Aloe vera
Long hailed for its soothing nature on burns, aloe vera can be used for moisturizing skin too.

Lavender
History cites that both the Romans and Greeks used lavender in their baths centuries ago.

Basil
Fresh basil contains vitamin K, which is important for healthy bones and proper blood clotting.

Basil

"The experience of growing, picking and using herbs from your own garden has a positive impact on your mental health," says Seham. Caring for herbs is a satisfying way to create a positive sensory experience.

Sun-loving basil is delicious in meals, and some types have health benefits too, according to Weill. "Holy basil has properties that help relieve stress and anxiety," she says. "The leaves are used for many purposes and act as an adaptogen, which is a natural substance considered to help the body adapt to stress. Having it can improve mental clarity."

Lemon Balm

This fragrant green herb is part of the mint family and is simple to cultivate. "Known for its calming properties, it has a light lemony scent that can be wonderfully intensified by rubbing the leaves between your fingers," says Seham. "It has been used to improve sleep, reduce stress and anxiety, improve appetite and help with indigestion."

She adds that lemon balm is common as a tea and is also used in beauty products, such as lotions and lip balm.

Spearmint

Spearmint is a hardy herb that grows quickly and is also part of the mint family. "It is great to just smell the leaves, without even needing to make a tea, for an immediate soothing effect," Seham says.

Give spearmint access to plenty of light if you decide to try it as an indoor plant. When growing outdoors, plant it in a container or confined space to prevent it from taking over the garden.

Spider Plant

With light green foliage and plenty of leaves, spider plants are another low-maintenance selection. "They do well with humidity and actually can handle varying forms of light, but they do best with medium light," Keith says. "Sometimes people will put spider plants in their bathrooms to have a warmer, cozier feeling in the space."

Occasionally, spider plants grow offshoots that can be snipped and potted as new plants. If you want a plant that'll keep on giving, this is one to choose.

Spearmint

Lemon balm

Top 10 Hard-to-Kill Houseplants

Celebrate your love of nature with these hardy indoor plants

by **Kaitlin Stainbrook**

S **SOME OF US MAY NOT HAVE THE GREENEST OF THUMBS,** but don't let that stop you from enjoying all the benefits of houseplants. Not only do houseplants add living beauty to your space, they help purify the air, giving you a boost in both body and spirit. (Though do keep in mind that some houseplants are toxic to furry family members or children, so check *aspca.org* or children's health websites before incorporating greenery into your home.) These ten forgiving houseplants will flourish under the care of even the most forgetful of gardeners.

^ Geranium
☀ ☁ ⛅

A reliable and eager bloomer, even in winter, geraniums come in every shade of the rainbow and then some. If you want to add more than just color to your living space, explore the world of scented-leaf geraniums, which come in fragrances like pine, peppermint and nutmeg.
Why we love it: Geraniums are best left to their own devices. Water thoroughly, but only as needed, then sit back and enjoy the show.

❯ Philodendron
☀ ☁ ⛅

Add a subtle touch of burgundy or golden yellow to your living space with the wide, waxy leaves of philodendron. Try the varieties McColley's Finale or Prince of Orange for colorful philodendron that are low-fuss. This houseplant can grow quickly, though, so keep it well groomed by trimming it back, staking upright types or winding the foliage around itself.
Why we love it: There are two types of philodendron: vining and non-climbing, so it's a cinch to pick the type that best suits your space. It also accents other plants wonderfully.

Top 10

1 Philodendron
2 Geranium
3 Hens and chicks
4 Aloe
5 ZZ plant
6 Norfolk Island Pine
7 Christmas cactus
8 Haworthia
9 Carex
10 Medinilla

⌃ Hens and chicks

Whether it's a single blooming sempervivum or a whole container of these rosette-shaped succulents, they make for an impressive presentation. These tough little guys need bright light to survive, and just one of these plants will easily propagate many more. This succulent's only weakness is mealybugs, which can spread to other plants in your home if you're not careful.

Why we love it: No matter where or how you plant it, hens and chicks will always look orderly and snug in their containers.

⌃ ZZ plant

With no blooms when grown indoors and a slow growth-rate, ZZ plant doesn't have a lot of frills. But what it lacks in pop, it makes up in polish with its glossy green leaves and vertical, palm-like stems. Splurge a little and buy a mature ZZ plant at the outset and give this slender statement plant its best chance to thrive in the indirect light of an east- or west-facing window.

Why we love it: ZZ plant works with every decorating style, because it looks awesome in any kind of container from a woven basket for a bohemian look to a chic glazed container for a modern space.

⌃ Medinilla

Put a medinilla in a room and it will instantly demand everyone's attention with its broad green leaves and pink-then-purple blooms. Give this showstopper houseplant the spotlight it deserves with a heavy container and a south-facing window, then watch as it slowly grows to the size of a small citrus tree (depending on variety).

Why we love it: Medinilla cheers up any room with its bright pink flower clusters during the doldrums of autumn and winter.

❯ Aloe

Want the look of an agave plant on a much smaller scale? Try family-friendly aloe. This funky-looking succulent flourishes in south-facing windowsills where they can get plenty of bright light, but east- and west-facing windows work just as well. Aloes love company—cluster a few different varieties together in one container for a unique look.

Why we love it: The popular aloe vera doesn't just look good—it will make you feel good too. The jelly-like pulp inside its leaves is a great home remedy for minor burns and insect bites.

‹ Carex
☀ ☁ ⛅

There are thousands of species of carex and they come in all shapes and sizes, but you really can't go wrong with any of them. You'll enjoy their elegant bursts of sweeping grass-like blades. If planting a larger variety, such as Ice Ballet (*C. morrowii*), you will eventually need a hefty container, but always start with a pot one size bigger than it is currently growing in to prevent root rot. **Why we love it:** If you have a habit of overwatering plants, carex is more tolerant of accidental soakings than most houseplants.

⌃ Norfolk Island pine
☀ ☁ ⛅

Create an evergreen forest in miniature with a few Norfolk Island pines. The soft, feathery needles make this live tree friendlier than most. It'll eventually become a small tree, but slow the growth process a little bit by keeping it tightly potted. Grow it in bright light and keep the soil moist. **Why we love it:** Although unable to hold heavier ornaments, Norfolk Island pine can pull double-duty as a Christmas tree. Think cute, homemade popcorn chains, origami and garland.

⌃ Christmas cactus
☀ ☁ ⛅

There are very few plants that prompt warm, fuzzy feelings of holiday nostalgia like the Christmas cactus. This cactus bursts into beautiful bloom in midwinter, and its plump flowers come in a range of colors from bright yellows to deep pinks. For the best performance, don't fuss and fret over Christmas cactus beyond watering it when its soil is dry. **Why we love it:** This cactus asks for next to nothing from its caretaker and will readily live on for years and years.

⌃ Haworthia
☀ ☁ ⛅

It's easy to guess why haworthia is sometimes referred to as the zebra plant—the white, stripey bumps along its leaves make it stand out in a crowd. Not only is this houseplant eye-catching, it also withstands nearly any abuse thrown at it, since it doesn't require much watering and does fine in most light conditions, though a south-facing window is best practice. **Why we love it:** European explorers brought haworthia back from Africa in the early 1600s.

A Taste of Summer

Grow a windowsill full of fresh herbs to add flavor to winter meals

by Niki Jabbour

I AM GOING TO LET YOU IN ON A LITTLE SECRET: Having a buffet of fresh herbs such as basil, oregano and parsley is the easiest way to elevate your cooking and add bright flavor to your food. It's also cost-effective because most herb plants are readily available and inexpensive—plus, they produce new growth for months.

Sourcing Herbs

Herbs like basil, parsley and chives can easily be grown from seed, but for an instant indoor garden, buy plants from your local supermarket or garden center. Certain types—mint, thyme and rosemary—may take months to size up when grown from seed, so starting with good-sized specimens means you get to start enjoying herbs right away.

Keep your green thumb thriving in any season when you grow herbs indoors. Thyme (far left) and basil are nearly foolproof.

Give herbs and indoor edibles a boost with this LED light kit from Gardener's Supply.

Let There Be Light

Providing enough light is the biggest challenge when growing herbs indoors, especially in winter. Many common herbs originate from warm regions like the Mediterranean and require plenty of light for healthy growth and large yields. "You can sometimes get away with growing easy herbs indoors in spring and summer months without grow lights if you are lucky enough to have a big, unobstructed south-facing window," says Leslie F. Halleck, author of *Gardening Under Lights, Plant Parenting, and Tiny Plants,* noting that even a bright windowsill may not provide enough light for sun lovers like oregano and basil. "I usually recommend sticking with part-sun, part-shade herbs like mint, parsley and cilantro indoors."

Since the goal of growing herbs indoors is to get a good harvest, Leslie suggests using grow lights to supplement natural light or to provide all light if growing away from a window. "By using one or two full-spectrum LED grow lamps in the 20-to-45-watt range, you can provide adequate light for your herbs," she says. "If you are providing only supplemental light, run the grow lamps for three to six hours a day; if you are providing all the light, run them for 12 to 16 hours a day."

Getting Moisture Just Right

Herbs need enough water to keep their roots adequately moist, but not so much that they rot. My kitchen windowsill is the most convenient spot to grow herbs because it lets me keep a close eye on soil moisture. Not sure when to water? Stick a finger in the soil. If it's dry, water. If it's moist, don't water.

Rosemary

Troubleshooting Tips and Tricks

Before you find an indoor home for herbs, do a quick scan. "Keep plants away from heating elements or vents that could cause plants to dry out too quickly," says Leslie, who also mentions that low indoor humidity in winter can be a challenge. Place pots over a drip tray filled with pebbles and water to easily increase humidity, especially in winter.

It's also a good idea to monitor for pests. "Spider mites, whiteflies, fungus gnats and aphids can be a problem, especially if herbs are stressed and not getting enough light or water," Leslie says.

Harvest Often

Never shy away from harvesting. The general rule is the more you pick, the more you get. Regular clipping encourages bushy growth, which means a bigger harvest.

5 Best Herbs to Grow Indoors

Many culinary herbs grow well indoors. Plant the ones you use the most.

1. Parsley. This is a great choice for a sunny windowsill where no supplemental lighting is available, as it can produce a good harvest in less light. Parsley adds bright flavor to pastas, soups and salads.

2. Oregano. Sun-loving oregano offers the best harvest when it's given plenty of light. In spring and summer, a bright south-facing window should provide enough light. In autumn and winter, add a grow light.

3. Thyme. The tiny leaves of thyme add big flavor to soups, stews and marinades. It's also very easy to grow on a south- or east-facing windowsill. For a flavor twist, plant a pot of lemon thyme.

4. Rosemary. A popular indoor option, rosemary is a Mediterranean herb that needs full sun and well-draining soil. It's hard to replicate these conditions, but I've had success by supplementing with a grow light. I don't overwater, but I do mist daily. (Keep a decorative hand sprayer on the windowsill as a reminder.)

5. Basil. The spicy-sweet flavor and aroma of basil have made it a top kitchen herb. Harvest often, pinching back to a fresh set of leaves to stimulate new growth.

Because I use certain herbs, like basil, a lot, I have been guilty of overharvesting from my plants. If your herbs are starting to look sparse, that's OK! Just buy a new plant. I like to keep two or three basil plants on my windowsill so I never run out of aromatic basil for my pasta sauces.

An Edible Oasis

How to grow potted fruit trees indoors

by Wendy Helfenbaum

YOU DON'T NEED A SPRAWLING ORCHARD in your backyard to grow fruit. You just need plenty of sun and indoor space, plus some patience. Laurelynn Martin and Byron Martin, authors of *Growing Tasty Tropical Plants in Any Home, Anywhere* and co-owners of Logee's Plants for Home and Garden in Danielson, Connecticut, offer some expert tips.

Light It Up

Most fruit trees—even the more shade-tolerant ones—need at least six to eight hours of direct sunlight per day to produce a crop. A large, unobstructed south- or west-facing window is an ideal spot for a potted tree. If you don't have enough natural light, look into grow lights.

Room to Grow

When planted in the ground, fruit tree roots spread out to find water and nutrients. But most potted plants do fine in plastic containers, notes Byron. Just make sure your pot is large enough to allow for growth and has drainage holes, as water buildup can cause root rot.

"Plants that are susceptible to root diseases are best grown in terra cotta pots," Byron adds.

Fill containers with standard potting soil mix and add plant-specific fertilizer regularly.

Keep Them Happy

Water fruit trees when the soil becomes dry on the surface, making sure to saturate the potting mix. If possible, keep your home's humidity around 50% for best results.

Byron also suggests pruning to maintain the

trees' sizes and forms while being careful to not cut off the flowering growths.

Choose Wisely

Larger temperate fruiting trees, such as apple, cherry, pear and plum, belong outside, says Byron. They require chilling time and plenty of height and room to bear fruit. Instead, he recommends selecting tropical or subtropical fruiting plants that'll be happy indoors.

Citrus

Byron says citrus trees, such as kumquats, are great plants for indoor gardening because they produce fruit very early in their growth.

Lemon and lime are two easy picks for beginners. Meyer lemon trees are quite hardy, and their fruit has more flavor than grocery store versions. Lime leaf and Key lime trees also yield quick crops.

Arabica Coffee

Try growing your own coffee beans! Laurelynn says coffee plants tolerate lower indoor light than most other fruiting plant options.

"The cherries, or coffee beans, are green before they ripen to red," she says. "Then you can shuck off the fleshy pulp and get the raw coffee beans inside."

She suggests storing the beans in the freezer until you have collected enough to roast for a cup of coffee.

Lemon Guava

Lemon guava (*Psidium littorale*) is a tropical plant that does quite well indoors.

"It tolerates the dry air and lower light found in homes, has shiny leaves and begins to fruit at 3 feet," Laurelynn says.

Wait for guava to turn completely yellow before enjoying its sweet flavor.

Tree Tomato

Originally from South America, this plant produces egg-shaped red fruit that have a custardlike texture. The plant, which is sometimes called tamarillo, will fruit from late summer through the winter.

It does well indoors and is best grown from a cutting, according to Laurelynn.

Nagami Kumquat Tree

Tree tomato

Yellow cherry coffee

Head Outside

Once danger of frost has passed in your area, your fruit trees can enjoy the outdoors and the beneficial insects that will pollinate them. Byron points out that it's important to move the plants slowly. Put them in shade or partial shade first so the leaves don't burn, and let them harden off for a few days.

Mushroom Magic

Indoor kits put the "fun" in fungi

by Jill Staake

A **FEW YEARS AGO,** mushroom-growing kits exploded onto the market, and now people can't get enough! Here's how to get in on the "shroom boom" trend.

Why Mushrooms?

"People are used to watching a plant sprout from seed and grow, but they rarely pay attention to the fungus life cycle," says Matt McInnis, co-founder of North Spore, a mushroom supply company based in Maine. "Mushrooms grow in niche environments that other food plants don't tend to tolerate."

Mushrooms' fast growth rate means your crop is ready to harvest much sooner than with tomatoes or beans. Plus, they're a great source of protein and nutrients, as well as easy to grow right at home.

Kits Make It Simple

Start with one of the many kits available on the market today. "These kits focus on species of mushrooms that aren't finicky and will grow in most environments," Matt says.

Many of the beginner kits use oyster varieties. The kits usually include a log or sawdust block that is pre-colonized with mycelium (the mushroom's root system) and mushroom spawn, which remain dormant until you open the container and provide water and indirect light.

Know How to Grow

Spray the growing kit with water a couple of times a day, and keep it in a humid area that's out of direct sunlight—near your kitchen sink can be ideal. Contrary to popular thought, mushrooms

don't grow in complete darkness, but bright sun does cause them to dry out. Within a week or so, you'll see small "pins" begin to form, aka baby mushrooms. A couple of days after that, your mushrooms will be ready to harvest!

Want to skip the kit? You'll need a bucket, a sterile growing substrate and mushroom spawn. Follow the growing directions for your specific variety, and the fungi will be ready to eat in no time. "Mushrooms want to grow," Matt says. "All you need to do is pay a little attention to their environment."

Expand Your Harvest

Along with the popular oyster varieties, indoor growers can also try lion's mane, shiitake, wine cap and button mushrooms. When you're ready for more of a challenge, take on reishi, maitake or morels. These often require some advanced techniques and equipment, such as specially designed fruiting chambers known as "Martha tents," and they may take a little longer to yield a harvest.

Whether you invest in a kit or try your luck from scratch, growing mushrooms indoors is a rewarding pastime. As Matt points out, "They're the missing link in our food system, and they are finally getting the attention they deserve."

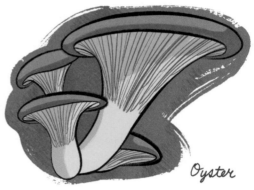

Oyster

Wine Cap

Maitake

Shiitake

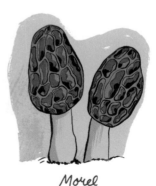

Morel

Quite the Arrangement

Grow these easy-care, long-lasting flowers for DIY bouquets

by LUKE MILLER

‹ Gladiolus

GLADIOLUS SPP., ZONES 8 TO 11

This stately flower reaches 2 to 5 feet tall and grows from a corm that can be overwintered in cold climates and replanted each spring. Eye-catching tubular flowers come in many colors, such as yellow, pink, white, purple and more, and sit on elegant spires. To ensure a longer blooming season, sow successive batches of corms 10 to 14 days apart.
Why we love it: A stalk of gladiolus looks majestic in the garden and adds height to bouquets inside.

⌃ Allium

ALLIUM SPP., ZONES 4 TO 9

A garden with alliums, particularly a large cultivar such as the Globemaster, has instant, whimsical appeal. The showstopping flowers are a beautiful sight at peak bloom, then hold their shape to become pretty dried flowers. Some gardeners even spray-paint the dried flower heads to give them a lasting color.
Why we love it: The one-of-a-kind blooms pop in a variety of shades, including burgundy, lilac, yellow and white.

⌃ Ranunculus

RANUNCULUS SPP., ZONES 8 TO 11

Also known as Persian buttercup, ranunculus flowers during the cool months of spring. Its blooms feature a wide range of colors, including apricot, yellow, orange, burgundy, white and romantic pastels. The sturdy stems and light fragrance makes it a florist's favorite.
Why we love it: The roselike blooms are tightly packed with gorgeous tissue-thin petals.

‹ Cosmos

COSMOS BIPINNATUS, ANNUAL

A popular self-seeder, cosmos is easy to sprout—and easy to spot, thanks to a plethora of bright white, yellow, orange, red or pink flowers. The three B's (birds, butterflies and bees) adore the bright blooms too. Cosmos plants range in height from 2 to 6 feet, depending on species, and are tolerant of poor, dry soils.
Why we love it: Ferny foliage adds a textural contrast to the garden and is a fine foil for clusters of flowers.

⌃ Dahlia

DAHLIA SPP., ZONES 8 TO 11

Dahlia is *the* cut flower for those who like variety. Not only does it come in a wide range of colors, but this tuberous root also boasts an assortment of flower forms, including pompoms, cactus and peony. A type called the dinnerplate dahlia has flowers up to 15 inches in diameter. Compact dahlias grow only 18 inches tall, while others reach 5 feet or higher.

Why we love it: No two types of dahlias are the same, so a cultivar exists for everybody's taste.

⌃ Mexican sunflower

TITHONIA ROTUNDIFOLIA, ANNUAL

Although the species can reach 6 feet tall and may require support, shorter cultivars bred from this Mexican native flower are much more manageable at 2 to 3 feet in height. The zinnialike blooms, which draw butterflies, are usually bright orange with a golden center, but some cultivars sport other warm hues.

Why we love it: Enjoy bright bursts of orange in a vase with some added wire support.

❮ Gloriosa daisy

RUDBECKIA HIRTA, ZONES 3 TO 8

This short-lived perennial or biennial is related to the garden classic, black-eyed Susans. Gloriosa daisy grows 1 to 3 feet tall and blooms in summer and fall. This wildlife-friendly plant welcomes bees, butterflies and birds, such as finches, that pick at the seeds.

Why we love it: This tough, brightly petaled prairie plant reseeds readily and blooms for months.

⌃ Zinnia

ZINNIA ELEGANS, ANNUAL

A cheerful annual for sunny gardens, zinnia offers a smorgasbord of colors. Zinnias go from seed to bloom in just two to three months, offering long-lasting flowers from summer till frost. Butterflies adore them, so plant zinnias in drifts for the best effect.

Why we love it:
Newer zinnia cultivars are the perfect option for gardeners who have previously lost zinnias to powdery mildew.

⌃ Celosia

CELOSIA SPP., ANNUAL

Depending on the species, celosia flowers take different shapes, such as the plumes above. Colors include maroon, red, purple, orange, chartreuse and white. The mature height is between 8 and 36 inches. Grow in the front or back of borders, based on the height of the plant.
Why we love it: Celosia is easy to grow and lasts two to three weeks as cut flowers. The flowers also look great dried. Just hang in a cool, dry place for a few weeks.

❮ Rose

ROSA SPP., ZONES 2 TO 9

The king of flowers—in the garden or in a bouquet—roses earn their title with a mix of colors, shapes and fragrances. Fortunately, some varieties need less care than others, particularly hardy shrub roses.
Why we love it: A dozen roses from the florist is an expensive treat, but homegrown roses are less pricey and can last two weeks or more in a vase.

Sunflower Bouquet

Get inspired by Vincent van Gogh with this pretty-as-a-painting seasonal arrangement

Supplies

12-in. vase with tapered neck

Floral preservative (optional)

Pruners or clippers

6 full stems of Hot Biscuits amaranth

5 stems of ProCut Bicolor or other bicolor sunflowers

6 stems of Chocolate or other dark sunflowers

8 branching stems of rudbeckia, such as Cherokee Sunset mix

8 stems of rudbeckia, such as Chim Chiminee mix

15 stems of millet (*Setaria macrostachya*)

Directions

Step 1: Fill the vase three-quarters full with water. Mix in floral preservative. Place the brown amaranth stems in the vase, cutting some shorter and leaving some longer, encouraging them to cascade over the edges so they create a loose foliage frame for the other ingredients.

Step 2: Add the bicolor sunflowers, nestling them in among the amaranth.

Step 3: Weave in the dark sunflowers, filling in the spaces between the amaranth and other sunflowers.

Step 4: Add the branching Cherokee Sunset rudbeckia evenly throughout the arrangement so they arch out over the sides of the bouquet.

Step 5: Thread in the Chim Chiminee rudbeckia, filling in any remaining holes in the bouquet. These spiky blooms add an airy element that breaks up the heaviness of the other, chunkier ingredients.

Step 6: Place the millet throughout the bouquet, making sure the small-flowered seed heads are high enough above the other stems to be seen.

Excerpted from Floret Farm's Cut
Flower Garden by Erin Benzakein
with Julie Chai and photographs by
Michèle M. Waite. © 2017 by Erin
Benzakein. Reprinted courtesy of
Chronicle Books. All rights reserved.
Photos: Michèle M. Waite for
Chronicle Books

Easy Ways to Dry Flowers

Create everlasting bouquets and decorations by preserving summer blooms

by Sally Roth

Make It!
Set hydrangeas in a vase without water. Once they're dry (this will take about a week), attach the stems to a wreath form with floral wire.

DRYING FLOWERS IS EASY—it's remembering to actually cut them that is a challenge. Just before your favorite flowers reach their peak, think about how you might use a dried version of them, whether it's for classic indoor wreaths, arrangements or other decor.

Pick flowers for drying in the early afternoon on a sunny day, when their water content is lowest. Collect blossoms right at their peak—any older and the petals may drop as they dry—and play around with these simple drying methods.

Forget the Water

If you've ever forgotten to add a little extra water to a vase, you may have already succeeded at the easiest method of drying flowers—simply deprive them of water. Now do it deliberately! Clip a small handful of stems, remove any leaves, and put them loosely in a vase without water. Even huge dinnerplate dahlias dry in about one week.

Hang Tight

The stems of some flowers may droop before drying if you leave them standing in a waterless vase. Keep blooms' upright posture by hang-drying them. Tie several stems together with twine or a rubber band and hang the bunch upside down away from sunlight, which fades the blossoms. They will dry in a few weeks.

Speedy Silica Gel

Moisture-absorbing silica gel requires a little more effort than other methods, but flowers dried this way look more like their fresh versions, with their natural shapes and colors preserved.

To get started, buy a tub of silica gel crystals at any craft store, and find a microwave-safe container with a lid.

Clip off all but an inch of the flower stems. Pour a 1-inch layer of the crystals into the container. Place the fresh flowers right-side up on top and add another 1-inch-deep layer of crystals. Snap on a tight-fitting lid, wait two to five days, depending on the size and thickness of the flowers, then carefully uncover your buried treasure and shake off any loose crystals.

Speed up the process by microwaving the dish, uncovered, for a couple of minutes on medium power. The time varies, depending on flower size and the wattage of your microwave, so feel free to experiment with it.

Once the blooms have reached the dryness you desire, remove the dish from your microwave (caution: hot!), snap on the lid, and let cool before opening it again.

Attach a wire stem to the blooms or glue them into place on a wreath, in a shadowbox, or wherever you want to show off your newly preserved flowers.

Whichever method you choose, summer is the time to start making new memories. That's when blossoms are reaching their peak. The garden is brimming with beauties to dry, ultimately allowing you to enjoy them indoors all year.

Best Blooms for Drying

Vase dry

Baby's breath

Dahlia, multi-petaled types

Geranium (*Pelargonium*)

Hydrangea

Pussywillow

Rose

Hang dry

Artemisia, foliage

Chive flowers

Globe thistle

Gomphrena

Lamb's ears, flowers or foliage

Larkspur

Lavender

Marigold

Oregano, flowers and foliage

Rose

Sage, foliage

Salvia

Yarrow

Silica gel

Black-eyed Susan

Coneflower

Dahlia, daisy types

Gerbera daisy

Pansy

Rose

Zinnia

Pretty Patterns
A bunch of celery cut about 2 inches from the base makes a large rose shape (shown below and above on packages). Radicchio (shown above on small cards) creates a striking single design.

Veggie Stamps

Pick a bunch of celery, a few carrots or some okra to make fresh patterns. Ready, set, ink!

Supplies
One or more vegetables
Ink pad
Plain wrapping paper or blank cards
Paper towels

Directions

Step 1: Cut the vegetable crosswise to reveal the cross section. (We used the base of a bunch of celery.) Stand, cut side down, on paper towels to blot up some of the excess moisture.

Step 2: Press the vegetable's cut side into the ink pad to cover the surface. Make a few practice stamps on scrap paper to work out how much ink is needed and how much pressure to apply.

Step 3: Lay a folded dish towel under the paper or card to be stamped. The layers of towel soften the surface so that the vegetable presses evenly into the paper. Stamp a repeat pattern all over the paper for gift wrap.

Step 4: Stamp a single image onto a blank card to create a matching tag.

Gardens Under Glass

Grow a personal paradise in only six simple steps

by Rachael Liska

THERE'S SOMETHING MAGICAL ABOUT TERRARIUMS. Maybe it's the idea of creating a tiny living world encased in glass, or because they enhance any indoor space, from boring offices to bedrooms. And terrariums are especially appealing when winter occupies the real world outside. Here's how you can make your own go-to happy place.

Dream a Theme

Create a beautiful biosphere by first considering the "landscape" you want to achieve. That landscape—say, lush rainforest or arid desert or mossy knoll—will dictate the kind of plants, container and decorations to use. Your goal is to simulate the perfect natural conditions needed to keep the plants thriving with little care.

Choose the Right Container

Most likely, you already have a clean, clear glass container you could use. Good options include a canning jar, fishbowl, vase, candy dish, cookie jar or pitcher. You can also find lots of decorative options at craft and thrift shops, home improvement stores and online. When considering a container, make sure that the opening is large enough to get your hands, plants and tools through. Terrarium containers fall into two categories:

Closed Terrariums: These are best for plants such as moss, ferns and aquatic plants that flourish in humidity. Because water tends to stay trapped and humidity is high, these plants can thrive with little care for long periods of time.

Open Terrariums: These are best for plants that appreciate dry conditions, such as cactuses, succulents and air plants. These plants thrive in low-moisture environments and prefer good air circulation. Open terrariums, however, tend to dry out more quickly, so you'll need to water more frequently.

Gather Tiny Tools

Make planting and caring for a mini garden easy by collecting the right tools. Consider a specially designed terrarium toolkit or make your own. Organize a case with tweezers, small scissors, fine-mist pump sprayer, fork and spoon, wooden skewer or chopstick, and small, stiff makeup brush or paintbrush.

Plant from the Ground Up

Assembling a terrarium is so easy, even a beginning gardener can attain beautiful results.

Step 1: Pour 1 to 2 inches of small pebbles into the bottom of your container to encourage proper drainage.

Step 2: Top with a thin layer of activated charcoal chips, which wick excess moisture, reduce odor and flush toxins.

Step 3: Lay down 1 to 2 inches of light, humus-rich planting soil—just enough to cover plant roots.

Step 4: Time to plant. Make sure to pair plants with similar needs. Place tall plants in back and don't overcrowd. Pat each plant down, making sure it is secure. Finish with a light watering.

Step 5: Add a few rocks, glass marbles, figurines, miniatures or shells to bring the little landscape to life.

Step 6: Brush any excess dirt from the glass and place the terrarium in indirect light, never in direct sun.

10 Terrarium Plants to Try

Air plant	Jade plant
Dwarf black mondo grass	Mistletoe cactus
Friendship plant	Nerve plant
Golden club moss	Starfish plant
Hens-and-chicks	Variegated philodendron

Care Tip

Once a month, give closed terrariums a breath of fresh air. Remove the lid for a few hours. Add a little water if condensation doesn't appear after closing it up again. This is an ideal time to check for wilting plants; promptly remove them and any other debris.

The Great Indoors

When it's chilly outside, it's time to go green inside. These gardening activities and crafts from 5 popular books are perfect for beating the winter blues.

by Deb Wiley

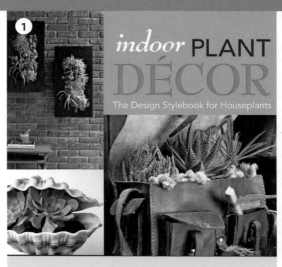

1. Make Corky Cute Planters

Turn wine corks into tiny planters with advice from *Indoor Plant Decor: The Design Stylebook for Houseplants* by Kylee Baumle and Jenny Peterson. "These miniature planters are cute as a button and never fail as conversation starters," Kylee says. "When using succulents, even watering is a breeze. The ones I made lasted a year, watering just a few drops once a month or so."

To start, drill a pilot hole about 1 inch deep in the top of each cork using a ¼-inch drill bit. Enlarge the hole with a ½-inch bit, taking care not to drill through the cork. Glue a magnet on one side to hang on a refrigerator, if desired. Add a tiny amount of potting soil, then tuck in a small succulent clipping. Add more soil if needed and gently tamp down. Colored aquarium gravel or moss adds flair above the potting soil.

Water 1 teaspoon or less every 10 days to two weeks. An eyedropper works well. When the plant grows too large for the cork, transplant it to a larger pot, take a clipping and begin the fun process again.

2. Multiply Plants with Moisture

In her book *Plant Parenting: Easy Ways to Make More Houseplants, Vegetables, and Flowers,* Leslie F. Halleck, a Dallas-based horticulturist, offers easy-to-follow directions for taking

Save wine corks to create crafty new homes for succulents.

cuttings, making clones and transplanting. "Once you catch the houseplant and gardening bug, you'll eventually want to make more of the plants you love," she says.

Water rooting is one of the easiest ways to make more plants. Start with a cutting from an existing plant or a large seed, such as an avocado, suspending it in a container of water.

You don't need to use clear glass to root plants, but it's fun to watch the roots develop,

2

A variety of container shapes and sizes work for rooting plants in water, including globe propagation vases (above) or test tubes (below).

Patented plants should not be propagated.

and you can see when the water needs to be changed. When roots are branched and 1 or 2 inches long, plant the cutting or seed in potting mix or continue growing it in water.

3. Grow a Garnish

Emma Biggs of Toronto, Canada, published her first book, *Gardening with Emma: Grow and Have Fun: A Kid-to-Kid Guide,* at age 13 (with help from her dad, Steven Biggs). She gardens indoors with microgreens. "Sunflower shoots are my personal favorite, with a delicious, sweet flavor," Emma says. "Pea shoots are popular, since they are crunchy and taste just like peas."

Other seeds to try include radish, kohlrabi, broccoli, cauliflower, cabbage, mustard, chia, buckwheat, and dried lentils or beans. To get a seed-starting adventure going, soak the seeds overnight. Next, find a pie plate or low-sided flat container, then add a layer of lightly moist potting soil and place the soaked seeds on top.

Lentil seeds are a great option for easy microgreens.

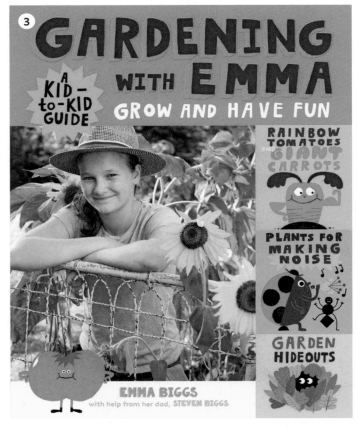

Put the plate on a sunny counter and wait a few days for roots to sprout. When the microgreens reach 2 to 3 inches tall, snip them off, give them a rinse and enjoy.

"In my house, we love to snack on fresh microgreens," Emma says. "They're amazing in salads, sandwiches, stir-fries and pretty much any other dish."

4. Test Your Memory

Sharon Lovejoy's creativity-sparking book, *Camp Granny*, explores the many ways to connect kids with nature. One is to make a memory game at home using natural materials simply photocopied to paper and cut into cards.

"This game is a double win," says Sharon. "You get to share time outdoors together and time indoors to craft your own unique nature cards."

Look for 24 different flat natural materials in your yard, then glue them on 3x5-inch index cards. Glue one item per card and let dry.

Place four of the nature-inspired index cards face down on a scanner and printer loaded with heavy card stock or photo paper; make two copies of each set of four cards.

Next, simply cut each copy into fourths for a deck of 48 cards.

To play, shuffle the cards, then lay them face down in four rows. Take turns flipping over two cards. Players who make a match take the set and get another turn.

Unmatched cards are returned to the rows face down. The game is over when all pairs are matched.

5. Harvest Again and Again

Katie Elzer-Peters, author of *No-Waste Kitchen Gardening: Regrow Your Leftover Greens, Stalks, Seeds, and More,* knows how to get extra use from her groceries. "Regrowing celery is one of my favorite no-waste projects because it's super easy, requires very little space and always results in another delicious harvest," she says.

Slice through an entire head of celery, about 3 inches from the bottom. Place the bottom—where the roots grow—in a clear glass container filled with 1 inch of water. Place the pot in bright but not direct sunlight, and change the water every few days. New leafy stalks will eventually emerge from the cut top.

Continue growing the plant in water, or plant it in potting soil that covers all but the new growth, keeping the soil moist but not waterlogged. Cut stalks as needed, but always leave a few to keep the plant going.

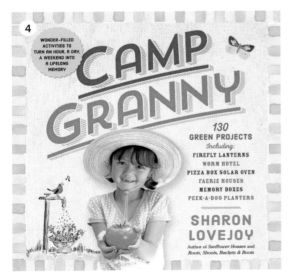

American goldfinches

Best Seat in the House

Indoor birding made easy

by Sally Roth

ONE VERY IMPORTANT consideration when it comes to setting up feeders is yourself! The better your view of the birds, the more you'll get to enjoy them. So instead of putting feeders way out in the yard, set them up just outside a window, no farther than about 15 feet.

Ultimately, the best seat in the house is wherever you can easily see the birds. "A feeder at the kitchen window can keep mealtimes interesting," says wildlife artist Heather Bartmann of Fort Collins, Colorado. Her main visitors are house sparrows, but even the most common birds are fun to watch if you can observe their behavior up close.

Remember to think of yourself first when taking care of your feeders. Make sure they are easy to access in all seasons, but especially in snowy weather when they will be busiest. Include larger feeders so you can go at least several days without refilling.

Try grouping your feeders on a multi-armed pole. That simple trick instantly cuts the cluttered effect of scattered feeders. It makes your assortment a single focal point, no matter what kinds of feeders you include, and ensures that you can see all of the action from your favorite window.

Nearly all backyard birds feel a bit uncomfortable out in the great wide open, where they're visible to predators. The temptation of a feeder will overcome birds' natural instinct to hide, but there's no need to put birds in danger. And, besides, when they feel safe, they visit more often and linger longer.

For sheltering cover, enhance your bird restaurant with cosmos, sunflowers and coneflowers or with berry-producing shrubs. As a nice bonus, those plants offer additional food that you don't have to buy!

Create a series of garden beds, shrubs or trees across the lawn so birds can hop, skip and jump from one to the next as they come and go from feeders.

Plant a small deciduous tree near the feeders for a landing zone. It'll get a ton of use in all seasons as an inviting place to perch. And it may entice grab-and-go birds like jays,

Northern cardinal

"A bird a hundred feet away is merely a bird, but within arm's reach it is an animated thing to marvel at."

Roger Tory Peterson
BIRD-LORE MAGAZINE, 1935

Get Started

Begin with a tube feeder to welcome finches, chickadees, titmice and cardinals almost immediately. Those species seem to recognize the shape of the feeder, and their presence attracts other birds.

chickadees, titmice or nuthatches to stop there instead of flying out of sight to hammer at their seeds.

The final trick: Create a window shelf, a simple board nailed to the sill, "to enjoy the birds at very close quarters," ornithologist Roger Tory Peterson urged 85 years ago in *Bird-Lore* magazine. After all, the benefits of bird feeding are for you just as much as for the birds.

Blue Jay

Even as the weather cools down, I keep my camera handy. I took this photo of a tufted titmouse from inside a garden shed that I've converted into a bird blind. I set up an area with branches and seeds about 20 feet from the shed's window. So that I don't disturb the birds, I keep the window closed and use a webcam to keep an eye on my photography subjects. That way, I'm ready to snap the shutter at the perfect moment.

Lucian Parshall
BRIGHTON, MI

We were lucky enough to have two male scarlet tanagers in our backyard for about a week last May. They spent most of their time feeding on suet, oranges and grape jelly—they weren't evasive at all. I caught this photo of one of the males flying by my office window.

Rodger Boehm
WINNETKA, IL

While working on my computer, I noticed a flurry of activity at the top of our cedar tree. A flock of cedar waxwings was devouring the berries. I ran to get my long lens and tripod and carefully opened the window. I knelt down so the birds couldn't see me and took pictures of them. It's hard to get a good photo of a cedar waxwing because they are usually high up in the trees. However, from the second floor of our house, these beautiful birds were very close.

Mary Lundeberg ENGLEWOOD, FL

I'm someone who would rather be outside when the mercury drops, especially when everything is wonderfully blanketed in snow. The air is crisp and there is a beautiful silence—until a blue jay's raucous call breaks the stillness, alerting other creatures to my presence. I have often called blue jays "the woods patrol."

Doug Dearinger FRANKFORT, KY

This young

sharp-shinned hawk looked right at me when I walked into my kitchen. I scrambled for the camera, switched the settings, made sure I had a memory card loaded and snapped this photo through a double-pane window. I'm so happy the hawk didn't fly away—and that I had washed the windows the day before!

Jacqueline Milburn
BOYCE, VA

Beyond the

feeders outside my picture window, birds perch on the crepe myrtle tree waiting to descend on a feeder. So this common grackle's menacing look was actually just a downward stare at the feeders. I took the photo in early March when bare branches provided a clear shot.

Suzanne Wright
WEST POINT, VA

It was an extremely rare opportunity to get a shot of a spotted towhee in the tree outside of our kitchen window. Since towhees are ground feeders, this just doesn't happen often. The male almost seemed to be posing for me on this particular occasion.

Douglas Edmiston
VANCOUVER, WA

This beautiful

Steller's jay found a hiding spot in a tree outside my kitchen window to wait for the peanuts that I put out each morning. I got this great shot as it poked its crested head out from behind the leaves.

Lorry Sue Turriff
COTTAGE GROVE, OR

A territorial eastern bluebird attacked its reflection in my office window, so I raised the window and captured this image between assaults. The bird clearly wasn't happy about it—right after its photo session, it found a different window to strike.

Bob Timmerman MURFREESBORO, TN

When I snapped a picture of this house finch, it looked like it was posing just for me. I'm lucky enough to have a picture window in front of my crape myrtle tree, and I've put feeders and birdbaths right outside the window, so that I can sit and watch the birds. After reading a few articles on the *Birds & Blooms* website, I hung some half-cut apples from the tree, which the finches really enjoy munching on!

Patricia Cortez BENTONVILLE, AR

I took this photo of a yellow warbler singing its heart out when I started doing wildlife photography. Boy, you really need a lot of patience to get photos of some of these birds, but it was an awesome experience that spring. I used my Nikon D750 and 70-200 mm lens.

Martin Torres
PORT HURON, MI

Surprise! A few years ago, a friend built the perfect woodpecker box for me, but the next summer, squirrels took over. I loved watching the cute baby squirrels get into mischief. But last year, new neighbors moved into the box— eastern screech-owls. I was absolutely ecstatic. When their baby was first learning to fly, it popped up in the window and nearly scared my pet cockatiel to death!

Kathryn Willet
BOYNTON BEACH, FL

CHAPTER 3
Natural Beauties

Amp up your gardening game by understanding the role pollinators play, attracting birds and butterflies, and learning planting strategies that lead to picturesque success.

Meet the Native Bees in Your Backyard

Plant your garden with bees in mind and help these powerful pollinators thrive

by Heather Lamb

Solitary bee

IN THE WORLD OF BEES, honeybees get a lot of attention. And right now, massive numbers of honeybees are disappearing. This phenomenon, known as colony collapse disorder, threatens both beekeeping operations and the pollination of crops and natural landscapes.

Although colony collapse doesn't impact native bees (honeybees originated in Europe), the possible causes behind colony collapse, such as pesticide use, habitat loss and disease, easily could.

Native bee populations are seeing declines, though not as widely documented as those of honeybees, says Mace Vaughan, co-director of the Pollinator Conservation Program of the Xerces Society. Among native bumblebees, 30 percent of species have experienced significant drop-offs that could lead to extinction.

Concern about colony collapse has brought attention to the critical pollination role of *all* bees and their plight, and also spotlighted what people can do to help, says David Mizejewski, a naturalist with the National Wildlife Federation.

To create a yard that's safe and attractive to native bees, it's important to understand them first. Here are four facts about native bees to help you grow a garden that's truly fit for these powerful pollinators.

All bees are being threatened right now, including honeybees and native bees, but you can take action to help.

Bumblebee

Bumblebee

Sweat bee

We rely on bees to pollinate flowers like this one. Remember, they pollinate all of our food that grows too.

Honeybee

1. They hide in plain sight. Native bees can look different from how we often visualize these flying insects. "Most of the things we learn about bees as kids aren't true about native bees," David says. They exist in an array of colors, including metallic green, brown, black and gray, as well as the stereotypical yellow-and-black stripes. Native bees can be quite small and are often mistaken for flies.

It's also useful to note that native bees tend to be docile. "Many can't sting humans," says Heather Holm, the author of *Pollinators of Native Plants*. "Their stingers can't even pierce our skin."

2. To find where they nest, look down. Most solitary bee species nest in the ground; the rest use tunnels, like hollow stems, or burrow into dead wood. Inside these nesting sites, the female bee creates a pollen loaf, lays a single egg on it, then starts a new nesting site and repeats the process.

To create a safe habitat for this type of nesting, it's essential to have areas of undisturbed and loose ground. Bees tend to select south-facing slopes with well-drained soil, which can be warmer and drier, and make for good nesting sites. Heather suggests forgoing mulch in spots where you'd like to see bees nest. "Many of the bees are small and can't get through a layer of mulch," she says.

When cutting back your plants in fall, leave behind foot-long lengths of pithy or hollow stems for the tunnel nesters; cavity-nesting bees will use those stems the next year. You can also create natural bee houses by bundling together hollow stems and hanging them in the yard. Fallen wood, brush piles or old fence posts provide good nesting sites as well.

3. Native bees are really busy—help them out. Most female native bees are active as adults for two to six weeks. During that time, they are collecting pollen to create as many loaves and lay as many eggs as possible. To make foraging for pollen less arduous, provide a diverse selection of flowers from spring to fall and plant them in groups.

New generations and different species of bees are emerging throughout the growing season and it's essential that they have enough flowers for pollen collection. Heather advises gardeners identify flowering gaps during the growing season and add plants to the yard accordingly. "Bees need that continuous succession of plants flowering," she says.

Honeybee

Concern about colony collapse has brought attention to the important pollination role of all bees.

Honeybee

Bee-Garden Basics

When gardening for bees, here are a few general rules of thumb:

- Choose a wide range of flower shapes and colors to attract the most bee species. Bumblebees can easily collect pollen from complex flowers, while smaller bees appreciate simple flower shapes and a flat place to land.

- Plant season-long blooms to support bees from early spring until fall.

- Provide areas of undisturbed ground or vegetation for nesting sites.

- Bees and flowers have evolved in tandem, so choose nonhybrid natives.

- Plant in masses for efficient pollen collection. Sunny areas are most attractive.

- Avoid pesticides. Surprisingly, even some organic mixtures can harm insects.

- Provide a muddy area or shallow trough for water.

If possible, plant flowers in masses about three feet across. "As bees are flying across a landscape, a cluster of flowers has a billboard effect," Mace says. "It's also efficient, allowing bees to visit many flowers rapidly."

4. Yes, native flowers are best. The relationship between bees and flowers is symbiotic—bees need the flowers for nectar and pollen, and flowers need the bees for pollination.

A flower might be specialized to allow pollination only from certain species of bees, or its structure might help assure proper pollination, Heather says. For instance, if nectar is deep in a flower, a bee will have to push its way into the flower to get at it. For a large, strong bee, like a bumblebee, this is an easy task and the flower deposits pollen on the bee in the process. A smaller bee might not be able to get to the nectar and will seek another flower.

Bring in a hybridized flower, like a cultivar that will display double blooms or a different

color, and who knows what effect that change might have on its pollen or nectar. "When we select cultivars of native plants, we don't know how that is affecting other attributes of the flowers that are important to pollinators and wildlife," David says.

In the name of attracting bees, it's best to choose heirloom plants or those bred as little as possible. For ideas, stroll through your local garden center and see what plants are covered with bees, Mace says. Some of the flowers he recommends are anise hyssop, bee balm, catmint, milkweed, penstemon, sedum and sunflower. But depending on the conditions in your yard, there are hundreds that will work. (You can easily find plant lists for different regions online.)

"The point is that everybody can do something for the bees and everybody can have something pretty," he says. "Plant the right flowers and avoid pesticides. Do that and you'll be rewarded."

Graceful in the Garden

Dragonflies nimbly dance through landscapes and parks during the summer months. Readers caught these serene moments of rest.

This cool little dragonfly kept trying to land on me while I was at Ravine Gardens State Park early one morning. I quietly waited for it to find somewhere else to rest so I could capture this photo.

Jim Bailey
EAST PALATKA, FL

On a hot summer day on my patio, I spotted this friendly dragonfly on my echeveria plant. The natural lighting was perfect, and my iPhone 11 Pro Max captured this amazing photo.

Kimberly Ward
DURHAM, NH

An August day found me at my favorite blackberry patch, which was practically dripping with fruit. I reached out to pluck a handful and froze when I saw this dragonfly sitting perfectly still. Camera in hand, I got as close as I could with time to take numerous shots. The beautifully colored body and the translucent wings surprised and delighted me.

Martha Lane
BELLEVUE, WA

As I enjoyed the visitors in the pollinator garden, this dragonfly landed on a spent coneflower. I love the way the sun highlights its wings. My kids and I were quite intrigued by this flier!

Diana Hudgins
SANDY HOOK, VA

Cool Dragonfly Facts
Surprising tidbits about these interesting fliers

- Dragonflies breathe using holes, or gills, which are in their abdomens.
- Tell the difference between a dragonfly and a damselfly by looking at the wings. Dragonfly wings point away from the bodies when at rest.
- Two pairs of transparent wings help dragonflies fly up to 35 mph.

I came across this very curious dragonfly on a chilly, damp day while at work. It was in the wet grass, and when I put my hand down, it crawled onto my finger— not shy at all! It seemed to like the camera, letting me take a few shots before it flew off. I think it warmed up from my body heat.

Paul Kneebone WOODLAND PARK, CO

Butterflies Worth Knowing

Carve out time to appreciate the beauty of butterflies. Take a look at our list of the most delightful and impressive species in North America, then get out there and see how many you can spot. Though they won't all be in your region, these fascinating fliers should be on your bucket list.

by Sally Roth

Monarch

It's the world's most famous butterfly. The monarch is renowned for its migration, when multiple generations work their way north during spring and summer, then a fall generation flies all the way to southern Mexico or to the California coast to spend the winter. Monarch caterpillars eat milkweed, absorbing chemicals that will stay in their system to make even the adults taste bad to predators.

Gulf fritillary on marigold

Gulf Fritillary

With long, narrow wings, big silvery spots and a pattern of black lines on orange, the Gulf fritillary is a high-fashion butterfly, looking elegant from any angle. Named for the Gulf of Mexico, you can also find it from the Carolinas to California, and it wanders far to the North. Gardeners can spruce up their yards and attract this flashy flier by growing its host plant: passion vine.

Cloudless Sulphur

North America has many kinds of yellow sulphur butterflies, and this is one of the largest. Males are pale yellow all over, while females vary from white to dull orange. Cloudless sulphurs are most abundant in the South, but every year in late summer they fly to the North, fluttering along through all kinds of open country, even reaching Canada.

Cloudless sulphur on thistle

Giant Swallowtail

Although some eastern tiger swallowtails are actually bigger, the giant swallowtail is usually considered to be our largest butterfly, spanning as much as five inches from wingtip to wingtip. Very common across the South, it regularly gets as far north as the Great Lakes and sometimes farther. Its caterpillars feed on the leaves of trees and shrubs in the citrus family.

Giant swallowtail on purple coneflower

Zebra swallowtail
on butterfly bush

Zebra Swallowtail

This ethereal beauty of a
butterfly flutters like a dream
through eastern forests.
Zebra-striped black and white
with accents of red, it features
long tails on the hindwings.
Adults that emerge in summer
tend to have even longer tails
than the springtime broods.
As caterpillars, they feed on
the leaves of a small tree called
the pawpaw, common in shady
woods, especially in the South.

Western
pygmy blue

Western Pygmy Blue

Butterflies known as blues are all small, but this one is absurdly tiny, measuring barely over half an inch across with its wings fully spread. There isn't room for much color on those wings, but a touch of blue shows up in flight. Usually considered to be our smallest butterflies, western pygmy blues are common in the West and Southwest, fluttering low over salt marshes, desert flats and even vacant lots.

Harvester

Harvester

A carnivorous butterfly? It sounds like something out of science fiction, but it's true. The caterpillars of this eastern butterfly are found on alders and other plants, but they're not eating the plants. Instead, they crawl around munching on aphids. Adult harvesters rarely visit flowers; you're more likely to see them chasing each other around the edges of alder thickets near streams.

Painted lady

Painted Lady

The most widespread butterflies in the world, painted ladies are found on six continents and many oceanic islands. They're also found all over North America, but not at the same time. In winter they're mostly in the Southwest or Mexico, but in warmer seasons they spread across most of the continent. Sometimes they make headlines, with millions flying above open country.

Mourning cloak

Mourning Cloak

You can find this big, distinctive butterfly throughout North America—and almost throughout the year. While most butterflies pass the winter in the caterpillar, pupa or egg stage, the mourning cloak hibernates as an adult. This means it could come out on warm winter days. Even in the North, it will fly during February thaws, and it makes a stunning sight as it glides through snowy woods.

Malachite

Malachite

Intensely tropical, the big, beautiful malachite flutters through the dappled light and shade of wooded gardens in southern Florida, and sometimes appears in southern Texas as well. When it lands, it shows off a scalloped wing shape and an elegant stained-glass pattern with panes of lime green and frames of chocolate brown.

Great Purple Hairstreak

Despite the name, it's not a
great big butterfly, and it's not
purple either. But it's larger
than most of the hairstreaks
(a group of tiny fliers), and it
flashes a beautiful blue when
it flies. Sitting still, it looks
mostly charcoal gray with
accents of red, blue, orange
and white. And its caterpillars
have specialized tastes—they
feed on mistletoe.

Be a Hero to Pollinators

Seven ways to create a paradise for bees, butterflies and other beneficial bugs

by **Erica Browne Grivas**

Eastern tiger swallowtail on native coneflower

JESSICA WALLISER smiles at the telltale slices in her coral bells' leaves. It's a sign that leafcutter bees are building their nests.

As a horticulturist and author of *Attracting Beneficial Bugs to the Garden,* she leaves perennials intact for overwintering insects and allows the wool carder bees to steal lamb's ears' plant fuzz. Her garden is a bustling and balanced ecosystem for bees and other pollinators.

Many gardeners are drawn to having an insect-friendly garden—not only because it offers a landing for garden helpers, but also because the plots need less water and pesticides, as well as less effort. Here are some simple ways to welcome back pollinators.

1. Fill in the Lawn

Traditional grass lawns reduce habitat and food sources for beneficial bugs and pollinators. Consider converting patches of your lawn from grass to flowers, shrubs or blooming ground covers. It looks fantastic and your garden will be easier to manage once established, notes landscape designer and author of *Prairie Up,* Benjamin Vogt. He says, "If the plants are layered and chosen correctly to match the site, they will require less maintenance than a lawn."

2. Use Eco-Friendly Pest Control

Jessica skips pesticides and instead attracts beneficial predators to get rid of unwanted visitors—for example, she attracts ladybugs to snap up aphids. If necessary, she moves to physical controls such as hand-picking or using row covers. Those methods take care of minor pest infestations and reduce

Bees on swamp milkweed

potential collateral damage to the helpful insects.

3. Add Natives

Native plant species "have coevolved with pollinators to produce the right nectar at the right time of year," says Jessica. They are a better choice than cultivars, which may not produce as much pollen.

4. Welcome Diversity

In wild spaces or gardens, variety in plants creates stability. Jessica says, "The more diversity you have in shapes, colors and structures, the more beneficial insects and pollinators you will have in the garden."

5. Redefine Weeds

"Sometimes the plants that are the most useful in attracting pollinators are the ones we call weeds," says ecological landscape designer Jessi Bloom, whose Washington garden buzzes with visitors to her wild yarrow, clover, fennel and even dandelions.

6. Plan for a Year of Blooms

Try to provide pollen for the entire growing season. Start the year with winter or early spring blooms such as crocus, heath and witch hazel, then transition to spring with phlox and columbine, and finish out fall with members of the aster family.

7. Do Less for More

Imagine less raking and pruning. When you skip these tasks on plants that can remain standing through winter, the spent stalks and patches of debris create homes for overwintering critters. So here's your mandate to leave the leaves.

Pollinator Pledge

- Grow pollinator-friendly flowers
- Provide nest sites for bees and butterflies
- Find pesticide alternatives
- Talk to neighbors about pollinators' importance

Front Yard Gardening

Once upon a time, front yards were just for show. They had a sweep of lawn, a few shrubs and maybe a hanging basket on the porch. Nowadays, this isn't the case at all. The front yard is becoming more and more lived-in, with gardeners sneaking in edible plants, adding gorgeous containers and creating amazing flowerbeds. Sound like your kind of scene? Take a look at these ideas for making the most out of your front space.

by Sally Roth

Daylilies line the sidewalk of this western home, and an arbor welcomes guests.

Create Privacy

Just because it's the front yard doesn't mean you can't have privacy. Put up an "open" fence that doesn't completely barricade your yard—spaced pickets, say, instead of high, solid boards—so it still feels welcoming. You'll feel sheltered from the public eye even though you're still visible on the other side.

Accessorize the Sidewalk

If you have a sidewalk around your house, use it to your advantage. Gardens along the sidewalk are a wonderful new trend, sharing beauty instead of keeping it all to ourselves in the backyard. Choose plants that can stand up to heat and dryness, like Russian sage, artemisia, threadleaf coreopsis and bearded iris.

Use Color

Flowers are still the place to start, and you'll want vivid ones in your front yard. Use bright colors that are visible from a distance, such as yellow, red, hot pink and white. This will help spotlight the entrance to your house. You can accessorize with pots and other items in these colors to tie in with your flowerbeds.

Add Front Yard Decor

Garden ornaments include any man-made object you can think of, from a classic urn to a painted wooden chair. These additions are powerful attention-getters, so use them sparingly. If you have too many, your yard will look cluttered instead of charming. Whether you follow the hottest new ideas or stick to timeless standards, your front yard ornaments give onlookers a sense of who you are.

Work on the Presentation

To give an ornament the spotlight, set it atop a pedestal—a recycled section of porch post, an inexpensive pillar from the hobby store or a section of clay drainpipe. If you love fairy gardens of dainty plants, moss and miniature decorations, put yours on a pedestal, so people can admire it without stooping over. Raising a container garden on an upside-down pot base boosts its allure too.

Incorporate Recycled Items

Move beyond ordinary lawn ornaments, and use your sense of humor. You might want to go for a literal garden bed—a headboard and footboard

If you'd plant it in the backyard, then it's fair game for the front yard.

Fencing in the front can be decorative.

Containers always add beauty and interest.

Paint a chair to add color.

Pathways invite guests in closer.

Recycle a bike for a unique touch.

with flowers as the coverlet. Check garage sales for objects you can repurpose as focal points in your front yard. For instance, you can build an entire garden around an old fat-tire bicycle. It makes a fine trellis for cypress vine, scarlet runner beans or other flowering vines.

Plant Edibles

Slip veggies into already maintained beds or into containers out front. The bonus of this method is you have less weeding to do overall. If you're wondering where to start, sow Swiss chard, lettuce of any kind, bok choy, kale and other greens in small patches in your flower beds. You can also punctuate your perennial bed with clumps of rhubarb.

Grow Trees and Berries

You might not think of trees and berries as front yard plantings, but they can be great additions. For instance, use a pair of dwarf fruit trees to flank your entryway. They'll have a lovely and fragrant show of spring flowers and you can look forward to the cherries, apples, apricots or plums to arrive. Another good fruit to try are alpine strawberries. They make a good edging to beds and borders. The runner-less plants stay in neat clumps, producing small berries of concentrated sweetness. When they're not blooming, they provide foliage.

Let It Go

Another trick to planting veggies in the front yard is to just let them grow. Plant asparagus behind your annuals. The spears you don't pick will turn to tall, feathery fronds that glow gold in fall. Indian corn is also a wonderful addition as an ornamental grass. Many herbs are good if you let them go as well. They offer excellent colors, lovely fragrances and they're pretty low-maintenance.

Take It Easy

Above all, you don't want your front yard to add a lot of extra labor, so plan ahead to keep chores to a minimum. Plant low-maintenance annuals and perennials, instead of those that need frequent fussing. Watering is the biggie, especially in sidewalk gardens, so rely on non-thirsty plants. Enjoy the view from your front porch, and don't forget to give a friendly wave if someone passes by.

Grow Your Own Grassland

Bring the prairie home with colorful
native plants that wildlife adore

by Sheryl DeVore

Build a prairie garden full
of black-eyed Susans and
other natives. Your space
will be low-maintenance
and wildlife-friendly.

A **TIGER SWALLOWTAIL BUTTERFLY** sips nectar from bee balm's purple blooms. A goldfinch snatches seeds from a black-eyed Susan. Indian grass sways in the wind. Whether you have a large space or a small one, you can re-create this native prairie scene in your backyard.

Prairie plants save time and money because, once mature, they require no fertilizer and no watering. "They're part of an ecosystem that keeps water clean and soils healthy, while providing native animals great habitat," says Laura Jackson, executive director of the Tallgrass Prairie Center at the University of Northern Iowa in Cedar Falls.

Prairie plants also are part of our national heritage, and it's important we do all we can to save them. Short-grass and tallgrass prairies once covered 600,000 square miles of North America. Now, less than 1 percent of native tallgrass prairie remains, Laura says.

Although you can start a prairie garden in spring, fall is a fantastic time too, because that's when seeds mature and scatter. Before you start, check local ordinances regarding height and location limitations of yard plants. Ask other gardeners if they have seeds to share, and don't forget to pay it forward when your own prairie becomes established.

Bee balm

Indian Summer black-eyed Susan grows in Zones 4 to 9.

Step One: Pick the Plants

Conservation areas and forest preserves sell native prairie plants in spring and fall. In autumn, gardeners often sponsor seed and transplant exchanges. "Just don't buy a prairie in a can, and if you go to a garden center, make sure you're buying straight species, not cultivars," Laura says. Go online or reach out to local nature centers to learn which wildflowers, called forbs, and grasses grow best where you live.

Potted flowers and grasses are good bets. They may be more expensive and need water the first year or two, but they help establish your prairie garden quicker than seeds, which can be eaten by wildlife before they have a chance to germinate.

Select species that don't grow much taller than 3 or 4 feet—perhaps 50 percent native grasses like little bluestem and 50 percent forbs such as bee balm and black-eyed Susan. In a few years, experiment with taller forbs and grasses.

Step Two: Choose the Spot

Give prairie plants what they want: lots and lots of sun. Pick a spot away from trees and other tall vegetation that could cast shade. Decide how much lawn or other vegetation you want to convert to a native prairie garden. Remember: Start small and expand later.

It's important to properly prep the area you've chosen. Benjamin Vogt, owner of Monarch Gardens, a landscape firm in Nebraska, started his prairie garden by removing part of his lawn. He cut sod into 1½-inch-deep strips with a shovel. Then he removed them, mulched the area and planted immediately. You can do as he did, or place a tarp on the lawn and weigh it down for about a month until the grass has died, although this may kill some beneficial microorganisms. Rake up any debris, then plant. Both methods can be done in either spring or fall.

Step Three: Start Digging

For seeds, use an 8-ounce cup of seed per square meter. Spread native grass seeds first, lightly raking the seed into the soil. Then scatter the wildflower seeds but do not rake them in. Scattering seeds just before it snows protects them from hungry birds. Some prairie seeds need to overwinter in the cold before they can germinate.

For established plants and seedlings, place tags by each one so you won't accidentally dig them up when weeding. Water as you would any other perennial. If you want to use seeds and established plants, scatter the seeds first.

Step Four: Maintain Your Prairie

New seedlings only grow a few inches in their first year. But mow taller weeds back to about 6 inches to keep them in check. After you've done this several times, you can stop. In colder climates, let snow blanket the seeded areas, wait for seedlings to pop up in spring, and follow the same mowing method. For transplants, keep the area weeded and water when necessary the first year or two.

Although some gardeners cut down stems and stalks of wildflowers and grasses after bloom time, leaving them up through the seasons provides food for birds and other wildlife. About every three years, mow your patch down to soil level in spring and rake off debris. Many grasses and forbs have deep root systems, so they will survive a mowing.

It might take several years for your prairie garden to look nice, so be patient. Also note that some plants spread like crazy—black-eyed Susan, for example. Just dig them up and share with your neighbors. Keep shrubs and trees in check so they don't shade out your prairie garden.

Step Five: Sit Back and Enjoy

A prairie garden is a mix of interesting leaves, buds, flowers and seeds that is visited by hummingbirds, moths, bees, butterflies and birds. In fall, grasses in some climates turn shades of gold, orange, and bronze, while finches and other birds perch on dead blossoms to eat nutritious seeds. Depending on weather and other factors, each season brings different sights and sounds to your prairie garden.

10 To Grow On

Check out these flowering plants and grasses. (They can grow up to 4 feet tall!)

1 Pale purple coneflower (*Echinacea pallida*)

2 Wild bergamot or bee balm (*Monarda fistulosa*)

3 Indian grass (*Sorghastrum nutans*)

4 Common milkweed (*Asclepias syriaca*)

5 Gray-headed coneflower (*Ratibida pinnata*)

6 Blazing star (*Liatris spicata*)

7 Little bluestem (*Schizachyrium scoparium*)

8 Black-eyed Susan (*Rudbeckia hirta*)

9 New England aster (*Aster novae-angliae*)

10 Prairie dropseed (*Sporobolus heterolepis*)

Garden for a Greener Earth

How to tend your garden in a way that's good for your landscape and the planet

by Luke Miller

HAVING A GREEN THUMB is a good thing. And helping the earth be greener in the process? Well, that's an even better thing. Here are the ways I've learned to be kinder to the environment when I'm in the garden.

Mulch with Care

Years ago, I mulched my front garden with dyed wood chips. The uniform color looked terrific, but when I dug beneath the mulch to plant, there was a spooky absence of earthworms. Although there's some concern about the dyes, the University of Florida Extension says the real danger lies with the wood, because it's sometimes recycled from treated or contaminated materials. Use natural wood chips instead. They are often available for free from local municipalities.

Leave the Leaves

As a kid, I earned money raking leaves for the neighbors. Back then, the leaves were sent to the dump. What a waste! Today, many communities collect and compost leaves. While that's good, I'd rather save money on bags and keep the nutrients in my yard. You can mow over leaves and use them to mulch beds. Or add them to your compost bin to help kitchen scraps break down faster.

Be Native-Minded

Tempting as it is to plant exotics you find at the nursery (many do make fantastic houseplants), your garden will require less upkeep with plants

Leaf mulch adds nutrients to the soil and cuts back on bagging costs.

Tomato seedlings sprout in peat pots, a sustainable alternative to plastic containers.

that are familiar with your growing conditions, so grow native plants instead. They're hardier, and need less water and fertilizer once they get established. As a bonus: Native plants are more useful to backyard birds than exotics.

Go Natural

A walk through the aisles at a big-box store will tell you how dependent we've become on pesticides and herbicides. Fortunately, more and more organic alternatives are showing up. Give these products a go instead (be sure to follow instructions), or forgo using any additives altogether. You can just pull weeds for peace of mind—and to know you're not killing one of nature's valuable pollinators.

Get Plastic-Savvy

Pots made of plastic are convenient, but it's hardly green to dump them in the trash after planting. When possible, buy plants in biodegradable peat pots. If you end up with plastic, repurpose it or recycle at a big-box store. I often start seeds in old cell packs and sink larger, used nursery pots into the ground to contain roots of aggressive plants like gooseneck loosestrife and other spreaders.

Put Nature to Work

The late Ruth Stout wrote a series of gardening books in the '70s on the benefits of mulching in place. This is called the Ruth Stout Method, and I can vouch for the fact that it saves labor, feeds plants and conserves soil moisture. The concept is simple: Mulch plants and beds with natural debris such as leaves, straw and pulled weeds. Then let nature do the rest.

American goldfinches
on tube feeder

Feeders for All

You can never have enough bird feeders. Learn about the different feeders available, and make plans to add a new one to your yard.

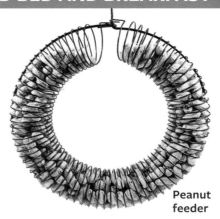

Peanut feeder

Hopper Feeder

The classic hopper usually has four sides, and it's common to find in the shape of a house or a barn. Sometimes you can even find options with suet feeders on either end. While it typically doesn't deter squirrels, it does offer a surefire way to offer black-oil sunflower seeds to birds of all sizes.

Tray Feeder

These types of feeders can either hang or sit atop legs on the ground. In both cases they are completely open, so birds have a big space to land and eat. Tray feeders are often used for larger birds like juncos or mourning doves. Some people who love squirrels even put out their corncobs on tray feeders.

Thistle Feeder

Often a tube-shaped feeder, thistle feeders hold the special thistle (nyjer) seed, which goldfinches love. Some thistle feeders are a simple mesh bag, while others are sturdier. You can even get some that are several feet long, holding dozens of goldfinches at a time.

Tube Feeder

If it's not a thistle feeder, other tube feeders have larger holes for seeds like sunflowers and safflowers. Often good squirrel deterrents, look for tube feeders that have a weighted contraption that closes off seed access when larger birds or squirrels land.

Suet Feeder

You can find more than half a dozen suet feeders on the market, including the classic cage design or the cage attached to a vertical wooden platform, giving woodpeckers a better way to perch with their tails.

Log Feeder

You can't get thriftier than taking an old log and drilling holes in the side. These holes are perfect for suet or straight peanut butter. Plus, the log gives woodpeckers and other birds a built-in perch.

Peanut Feeder

They're usually shaped like a tube, but you can also find peanut feeders in round, wreath shapes. These feeders have large holes, so the birds (and sometimes squirrels) have to work to get the peanuts out.

Sugar-Water Feeder

This feeder should be pretty self-explanatory. You can find it in a few standard shapes, and it's for those glorious little fliers we call hummingbirds. Keep in mind that a second sugar-water feeder (usually in an orange color) will also attract orioles and other birds.

Fruit Feeder

You can find a handful of other feeders on the market, including those that hold jelly or fruit like grapes, oranges and apples. These are great feeders to experiment with, especially in spring and fall, when you'll see the most migrants.

Downy woodpecker at suet feeder

Ruby-throated hummingbirds at sugar-water feeder

Baltimore oriole at fruit feeder

Triple Attraction

With traits that appeal to the big three—birds, butterflies and bees—these powerhouse blooms are top options for a wildlife-friendly garden. From easy-to-grow annuals to hardworking perennials, there's something for every landscape.

Cosmos

COSMOS SPP., ANNUAL

Throughout the growing season, bees and butterflies can't resist these colorful pinwheel-shaped blossoms with feathery foliage. Grow single or double cultivars of this easygoing bloomer in full sun, and you'll have flowers and seeds for the birds from summer through late fall. Plants stand from 1 to 6 feet high, so no matter how large your space, there's a type of cosmos that will fit right in.

Black-eyed Susan

RUDBECKIA SPP., ZONES 3 TO 9
Lovely as a background planting or in a wildflower garden, black-eyed Susan also shines when grouped with other daisy-shaped flowers. Plants range from 1 to 6 feet in height, offering a big visual impact in yards of any size. Butterflies appreciate the landing pad the blooms provide, bees flock to the bright yellow color, and birds love the late-fall seed heads.

Red admiral butterfly

Agastache

AGASTACHE SPP., ZONES 4 TO 11

Bushy and studded with blooms from mid- to late summer, agastache is a favorite of hummingbirds, butterflies and bees. Flower spires in pink, orange, yellow, blue or violet reach 2 to 6 feet high. Agastache thrives in full sun and in well-draining, fertile soil.

Coneflower

ECHINACEA SPP., ZONES 3 TO 9

Birds, bees and butterflies, such as fritillaries, truly love this perennial! You'll watch songbirds pause to nibble the seeds, and you'll see butterflies and hummers stop to sip the nectar into fall.

Bee balm

MONARDA SPP., ZONES 3 TO 9

This unusual beauty grows up to 4 feet tall and starts flowering in midsummer, inviting hummingbirds, butterflies and bees. Choose mildew resistant varieties for best results. Deadheading keeps this self-sower in check, but then you won't see songbirds stopping to eat the seeds once petals die back.

Blazing star

LIATRIS SPP., ZONES 3 TO 9

The nectar of this spiky plant is a butterfly favorite, especially when it comes to the silver-spotted skipper. After the flowers fade, birds favor the seeds. Blazing star reaches up to 6 feet tall, but some types, like Kobold, are much shorter, measuring roughly 18 inches.

Verbena

VERBENA X HYBRIDA, ANNUAL TO ZONE 9

Expect summerlong color from these blooms. The plant's stems spread out to about 18 inches. Keep the soil moist but well drained for optimal flowering. Verbena does well in containers, so use it to lure pollinators to small spaces.

Zinnia

ZINNIA SPP., ANNUAL

Zinnia is a butterfly and hummingbird go-to, but varieties of sparrows, finches and juncos eat the seeds later in the year. This annual is bee-friendly too, attracting honeybees, bumblebees and some solitary bees. It reaches up to 3 feet and blooms until the first frost.

Cabbage white butterfly on agastache

Verbena

Male ruby-throated hummingbird at bee balm

Honeybee on blazing star

Female ruby-throated hummingbird at zinnia

Aphrodite fritillary on coneflower

Say Yes to the Mess

Support backyard wildlife with a more laid-back approach to garden cleanup

by Kelsey Roseth

Leave sunflower heads in place to attract and feed seed eaters like northern cardinals.

MINDSETS ARE CHANGING about annual garden cleanup. Many gardeners work very hard after the growing season to ensure that their beds are pristine come spring, but experts recommend taking a softer approach to regular landscape and garden maintenance.

"Look at your garden through a different lens, and have less focus on complete tidiness. Think about what parts of the garden serve as habitat for wildlife," says David Ellis, director of communications at the American Horticultural Society.

Raking leaves, tidying beds and picking up debris from your yard could remove chrysalises, egg cases and the leaf litter that helps protect them. When you leave landscapes a bit unkempt, you provide food, shelter and nesting material for wildlife such as birds, bees, butterflies and other insects—and help them survive winter, their harshest season. Plus, when you keep organic matter in gardens or woodland, it decomposes and provides nutrients for the plants growing in your soil.

Let at least one area of your garden serve as a wild space, David advises. Even if it's only a couple square feet, local fauna reap the benefits. Create a small pile of leaves, sticks, stems and rocks for tiny insects seeking shelter. Leave ornamental grasses untouched until early spring. Dead flowers and leftover seed heads feed birds into fall and provide nesting materials for breeding pairs in the following year.

This approach might also help you zero in on your yard. "It reinforces the need for gardeners to take notes," David says. Keep detailed information on your

Brush piles give brown thrashers and other birds a spot to forage.

landscape to recognize year-to-year problems and create solutions for future growing seasons. You may notice that certain plants aren't a good fit for your space and should be removed.

Of course, some spots may still call for cleanup. Most vegetables have diseases that carry into the next growing season, and the dead leaves of some plants, like roses, are susceptible to fungal blight. Stop the spread by removing those types of dead plant material every fall or early winter.

The messy gardening movement is picking up steam nationwide. Some organizations, including The Nature Conservancy and the Cornell Lab of Ornithology, have even collected pledges from those who promise to be a little more lazy with their landscaping.

Annual Cleanup Checklist
Keep:
- Sticks and rock piles
- Dead leaves
- Flower stalks and seed heads

Remove:
- Diseased plants
- Dead annuals
- Vegetable garden debris
- Fallen rose leaves

DIY Bug Hotel

Create a place for your backyard bugs to put all six of their feet up and recharge their batteries

Supplies

Wooden frame
Plywood
Nails and glue
Sandpaper
Exterior paint
Drill
Rope
Twigs, bark, grass and leaves

Directions

Step 1: Build a wooden frame in any shape. Ours is a hexagon, but a square or rectangle will work too. Make sure it's deep enough so that you can add materials later—at least 3 inches should do the trick. If you don't want to build one, look for something to recycle. Try an old wooden drawer or a deep picture frame.

Step 2: Secure a plywood backing to one side of the frame with nails and glue. If the recycled frame already has a back, skip this step.

Step 3: Sand the frame and cover it with two coats of exterior paint. Choose a color that suits your backyard or complements the plants in the area where you plan to hang the bug house.

Step 4: To form a hanger, drill two holes in the frame, thread a rope through the holes and tie the ends together to form a knot.

Step 5: Fill the frame with natural materials. Stuff twigs, bark, grass and leaves into the bug hotel until it's full. Create plenty of small crevices for insects to hide and nest.

Step 6: Hang it and wait for your first guests!

A Team Effort
Before home-building begins, the male cardinal (shown here) follows the female around to potential nest sites. Once they find a suitable spot, the female starts building, while the male occasionally brings her nesting material.

Q Do cardinals build nests in birdhouses? If so, what height is recommended?
Joseph Duplessis
OSWEGO, NY

Kenn and Kimberly: Many birds that build nests inside holes in trees or other natural cavities, such as house wrens, bluebirds and tree swallows, take advantage of man-made birdhouses. Other birds, like cardinals, don't place their nests inside such enclosed sites, so they won't use birdhouses. Cardinals build compact, bowl-shaped nests of twigs, weed stems and strips of bark, wedged into a fork in a branch among bushes, trees or vine tangles. To invite a nesting cardinal pair, plant dense shrubs or short trees with plenty of low foliage—most cardinal nests are only 4 to 8 feet above the ground.

Q. How should I prepare birdhouses for winter?

Jennifer Broadstreet Hess
MARION, KS

Kenn and Kimberly: Some folks take nest boxes down in winter to make them last longer. We leave ours up for bluebirds; while many move south in winter, some decide to stay. Small groups often roost together in boxes, huddled for warmth. Our winter maintenance includes removing old nests, scraping out debris, and making sure the boxes are still sturdy and the predator guards are secure. If your boxes have ventilation holes, consider blocking those with weatherstripping. Just be sure to remove it in early spring to improve airflow.

Q. This egg teetered in a bluebird house. Is it a robin egg or a bluebird egg—and should we put it back in the nest?

Ashley Dobbs ARCADIA, MO

Kenn and Kimberly: What an interesting dilemma. This is a bluebird egg. We know it's not an American robin's because they don't nest in birdhouses, and their eggs are a little larger and a deeper blue. Since parent bluebirds make regular trips in and out of the box, it's unlikely that the egg had been sitting there very long. If there are other eggs in the nest, it won't do any harm to put it back in and see if it hatches along with the others.

Q What is the best way to attract bluebirds to my backyard, and where should I place the nest box?

Liza Peniston AUGUSTA, KS

Kenn and Kimberly: You can put out mealworms for bluebirds, but the best methods involve foods in nature. Bluebirds feed heavily on insects they find on or near the ground, so avoid treating your lawn with chemicals. During the colder months they'll eat mainly fruits and berries, so planting native trees and shrubs that bear fruit is a wonderful way to provide food. They also love birdbaths, and if you can make the water move—even if you just add a small dripper—that's better still. Bluebirds prefer large expanses of short grass. Place nest boxes in the most open area possible, away from your house or deep shade.

All in the Family

A male eastern bluebird attracts a female by drawing her to his nest site by fluttering his wings and carrying material back and forth through the hole. Once two bluebirds have paired up, the female builds the nest herself.

Q A wren won't leave a nesting pair of bluebirds alone. I installed a wren guard on the birdhouse, but is there anything else I can do?

Brenda Hagemann
WINSTON-SALEM, NC

Kenn and Kimberly: Wrens are native birds and we must not harm them, their nests or their eggs. No method is 100% effective, but here are some things to try, besides putting up a wren guard. If you have room, place your nest box in the most open, grassy area possible, at least 50 feet away from trees or cover. This is a bluebird's preferred habitat, and wrens are unlikely to nest in such open areas. Block the entrance holes of any purely ornamental (and unoccupied) nest boxes, as they could potentially attract more wrens.

Eastern screech-owl (red morph)

Q What is the ideal location and height for an owl box?

Kathy Lorigan EASTON, PA

Kenn and Kimberly: In your area, the owls most likely to move into a nest box are eastern screech-owls. They'll use boxes similar to ones preferred by wood ducks, at least 16 inches deep and with an entrance hole of about 3 inches by 4 inches. The box should be in a shady spot and about 10 feet above the ground. Fastening it to the trunk of a large tree may work, but in an area with many predators, it's best to place it on a tall pole that's protected with a baffle or predator guard.

CHAPTER 4

Enjoy Nature, Rain or Shine

No matter the weather, no matter the season—there's always an abundance of beauty in your backyard. Turn here for ways to discover Mother Nature's gifts all year long.

Feeding Birds 365 Days a Year

Switch up what you're serving to attract more birds to your backyard

by Ken Keffer

Don't forget about bird-friendly plants. Mountain ash trees attract a ton of birds, including this female pine grosbeak.

House finches and a cardinal eating seed.

I tend to notice the changing of the seasons by bird activity, not weather. When I see the first migrating sparrows return to my hedgerow, I know spring is on the way. And when juvenile birds are fluttering their wings and begging for food, it's summer. These sights can be huge hints that it's time to make some changes to your feeding routine. Follow this guide and you'll have a robust bird presence in your yard all year-round.

Winter

Even in the harshest of winters, birds can find plenty of natural food sources. But they will regularly hit up backyard feeding stations for a steady food source.

Foods that are higher in fat can give birds an extra boost. Try offering peanuts, either in the shell or without. In most feeders you can mix unshelled peanuts with sunflower seeds. Or you can feed peanuts separately. While the chipmunks are curled up for a long winter nap, you can bet the squirrels will be interested in peanuts all winter long too. (And so will the jays, chickadees and woodpeckers.)

Suet can be offered year-round, but in winter it's especially popular with woodpeckers, nuthatches, titmice and chickadees. Even odd visitors, such as pine warblers, may stop in to sample suet.

Attract steller's (shown here) and blue jays with peanut feeders.

Evening and pine grosbeaks and downy woodpeckers frequent feeders, especially during cold months in northern U.S.

Spring

With the arrival of spring comes the return of exciting migrating species. As these spring migrants start to arrive, you should enforce the spring-cleaning rule. Be honest—you didn't keep your feeders exceptionally clean over the long winter, did you? Cleaning your feeding stations regularly will help cut down on disease transmission and deter unwelcome visitors like raccoons.

As temperatures heat up in most of the country, it's the best time to hang nectar feeders for orioles and hummingbirds. These backyard favorites reach the Gulf Coast by late February or early March and will have made it northward by Mother's Day. You'll have the best success attracting orioles if you offer grape jelly or oranges in addition to nectar. Orioles aren't the only ones that have a sweet tooth ... er, beak. Gray catbirds, northern mockingbirds and American robins will also make special appearances at feeders in the spring.

Lastly, don't shy away from mealworms in the spring. They tend to be bluebird magnets, so if they aren't on your menu, give them a try. If you're not ready for live mealworms yet, buy dried ones. You might be surprised to see woodpeckers and chickadees stopping for mealworms too!

Woodpeckers, like this golden-fronted, enjoy a sweet treat. Attract them by putting out orange halves, grapes or mangoes.

Summer

The antics of young birds crash landing in the backyard will make anyone smile. It's easy to lure nesting birds to your yard by providing nesting material. Plenty of species use natural materials to line their nests.

It's important to be selective about what you offer, though. Most synthetic materials (and some natural ones, like cotton) can actually do more harm than good, especially when they're wet. Although commercial nesting material blends are available, you can create a buffet of natural materials for the birds by gathering up twigs, grasses or other plant material from your own backyard. Throw some of your pet's hair in there too. Some folks just toss materials around the backyard, while others use suet cages to hold the nesting material in place.

Another summer attraction is water. A birdbath is a nice touch, but moving water is even more irresistible to birds. Try adding a spinner, bubbler or fountain to your birdbath to see if it attracts any new guests. Water misters

are also an option. Hummingbirds have been known to dart in and out of the fine spray, preferring that to traditional birdbaths.

When it comes to serving food in summer, don't rule out suet. No-melt suet cakes are out there and they typically have more cornmeal in them, so they tend to be less of an oozy mess for those in the warmer climates. Nuthatches and woodpeckers will enjoy them even in summer.

Fall

Autumn is a season of movement for many birds. Migrants are headed toward their wintering grounds, but even local birds shift around in their ranges as they settle in for winter.

It's also harvest season in your garden, so let the birds do a little harvesting of their own. Leave your sunflowers and coneflowers alone and let the birds eat seeds straight from the source. Berry producers like dogwood, currant or bayberry can also attract fall birds. A flock of cedar waxwings might even devour all of the berries on your trees and shrubs in one quick, fall visit.

Yellow-rumped warblers sometimes visit feeders for seeds and suet, but they prefer berries, like this bayberry in fall.

As summer turns to autumn, many people take their hummingbird feeders down. Keep them up for a bit longer and you might be rewarded with a rare treat. Hummingbirds sometimes show up in unexpected places during fall migration. Rufous hummingbirds, a western species, are increasingly seen in the Midwest and East at this time. Other western and southwestern species like black-chinned, Anna's, Costa's and broad-billed have been reported far to the north and east in the fall. A good rule of thumb is to keep your feeder up for at least two weeks after you've last seen a hummingbird.

Feeding backyard birds can bring year-round enjoyment to your life. It will only take a short time for you to be more in tune with the changes happening around you. These seasonal patterns will become familiar and you will find yourself no longer marking the seasons by the weather, but instead by the birds.

Dried sunflower heads attract birds like white-breasted nuthatches.

Drought Busters

40+ plant picks that will help you beat the summer heat

by Sally Roth

HOW'S THE WEATHER? That might seem like simple chitchat to most people, but to a gardener it's the start of a serious discussion. After all, our beloved flowers are at the mercy of the skies. And every summer, we seem to be faced with hotter, drier conditions that can wreak havoc on our plants. Luckily, though, we have a wonderful range of adaptable plants to try.

What Is Drought?

Before we get to the plants, let's first look at drought. Usually dry spells are normal, because weather is variable. But when they continue week after week, month after month or even year after year, it depletes every bit of moisture in the soil. In short, you're dealing with a drought.

At this point, watering becomes an endless and expensive chore. Even worse, you might not be able to water at all if you live in a municipality that has drought restrictions. So what's a gardener to do?

Add plants! Well, this isn't quite as simple as it sounds. Sure, a drought mimics desert conditions, but in this case it's a temporary desert. Most of us need plants that can thrive in both drought conditions and wetter environments too.

This is why you can't just plant a bunch of cacti or agave. When the rain returns, their roots won't be able to draw up the

Backyard Tip

Whether your water is coming from the sky or from your hose, preserve that precious moisture by using mulch. A 2-inch layer of organic mulch will go a long way toward keeping the moisture in the soil.

Sedum

Artemisia

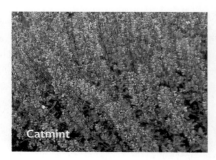

Catmint

extra water fast enough, and they may literally drown. The key is to have plants that can handle both: They can shrug off drought, yet they appreciate ample rainfall.

The Time Is Now

When's the best time to start drought-proofing your garden? Right now! Ideally, you want to get plants in the ground well before a dry spell hits. So there's no time like the present to hit the garden center and start adding drought-resilient perennials to your garden.

Don't expect them to work magic right away, though. Even the least thirsty plants in the

Globe thistle

Rock garden with sedum and California poppies

Blanket flower

Balloon flower

Yarrow

Dianthus

Hens-and-chicks

Gayfeather

world need moisture to get their roots established. Water your new perennials for a full year, while they grow the roots they need to weather a drought without skipping a beat.

What's Normal?

You probably have a good idea of what a normal amount of annual precipitation is like in your area. But many years aren't exactly normal. Besides, the precipitation report doesn't begin to tell the full story.

In my neck of the woods, on the dry side of the Rockies, annual precipitation is almost entirely snow. Come the growing season, the sky shuts off like a faucet. Week after week can go by with nary a drizzle, or at most a tease that barely wets the soil. It's a similar story in the Pacific Northwest, where winter is the infamous rainy season, followed by a long, lovely and usually dry summer.

Other parts of the country have a more balanced picture, with water falling year round as winter snow and summer rain. No matter what the usual cycle of precipitation is where you live, Mother Nature has a habit of throwing a monkey wrench into the works. So it's best to act like a Boy Scout and always be prepared.

Leaves Tell the Truth

Below ground, it's roots that help a plant get through dry times. Taproots go deep, as do the fibrous roots of many prairie plants, so they're able to draw up moisture even when the top foot of soil is bone dry.

Still, if a plant has big leaves or lots of smaller ones, even a very deep root will have trouble supporting the needs of the top growth. Hollyhocks, for instance, wilt very quickly in a drought, as do tomatoes.

So instead of examining the roots, be sure to take a look at the leaves, which are the main reason for water loss. Sun and wind, plus the normal process of transpiration through which plants breathe, cause water to evaporate. Roots are constantly working to pull moisture from the soil to replenish that supply.

Drought-tolerant plants have all sorts of defenses to prevent water from being lost through their leaves. That's why leaves are the No. 1 clue to how well plants will survive a scarcity of water.

Butterflyweed

Backyard Tip
One thing that drought-tolerant plants can't take is heavy wet soil year-round. If you have dense clay soil, either amend it or create raised beds.

Sea holly

Amsonia

Bearded iris

Creeping thyme

Salvia

If you have big green leaves an lush foliage, times will probably be tough when drought sets in. Small leaves and fewer of them? There's much less water needed. Leaves with a coating of fuzz or a waxy layer? These are great adaptations to prevent water loss.

Start Planting

Both the garden center and a local native-plants group are good places to find drought-resistant plants for your area. Be sure to check out our picks (at right) too.

It can take time to switch your plants over to drought-resilient varieties, but it's a good thing to keep in mind when adding new perennials to your garden. And it's a good goal to have in general. After all, if you get the right plants in place now, your garden will look glorious no matter how stingy nature is with water.

Drought-Tolerant Picks

We selected more than 40 plants that will thrive in climates that see both rain and drought. These plants, tolerant of difficult conditions, are often weeds or invasive in certain areas, so do some research before planting.

- Agastache
- Amsonia
- Artemisia
- Autumn sage (*Salvia greggii*)
- Balloon flower
- Bearded irises
- Blue flax (*Linum perenne*)
- Blue spirea (*Caryopteris x clandonensis*)
- Broom (*Cystisus and Genista*)
- Butterflyweed (*Asclepias tuberosa*)
- Candytuft (*Iberis sempervirens*)
- Catmint (*Nepeta*)
- Creeping phlox
- Creeping thyme; wooly thyme
- Culinary sage (*Salvia officinalis*)
- Dianthus, including Cheddar Pink and others
- Gaillardia
- Gaura
- Gayfeather (*Liatris*)
- Globe thistle (*Echinops*)
- Harebell (*Campanula rotundifolia*)
- Hens-and-chicks

- Ice plant (*Delosperma*)
- Lambs' ears
- Lavender
- Oregano, including ornamental-flowered varieties
- Ornamental grasses (non-invasive)
- Pine-leaf penstemon (*Penstemon pinifolius*)
- Purpletop verbena (*Verbena bonariensis*)
- Red yucca (*Hesperaloe parviflora*)
- Red-hot poker
- Rock rose (*Cistus*)
- Rosemary
- Salvia
- Sea holly (*Eryngium*)
- Sedum of any kind
- Sun rose (*Helianthemum*)
- Thread-leaf coreopsis (*Coreopsis verticillata*)
- Veronica
- Yarrow
- Yellow columbine, Swallowtail cultivar

Grow a Desert Oasis

Easy ways to combat drought, extreme temperatures and rock-filled soil

by Jill Staake

Gardening in arid climates can be a challenge, but the reward is evergreen color and plants with extraordinary shapes.

Found across the Southwest, prickly pear cactus supports wildlife, including nesting cactus wrens.

WHEN YOU PICTURE THE AMERICAN SOUTHWEST, you may see dusty, windswept deserts that stretch for miles, with a lone cactus and occasional tumbleweed to break the monotony. That's certainly one version.

Gardeners in the Southwest see another image—one that's filled with the beautiful blooms of hardy native plants, drawing hummingbirds and butterflies. They know it takes hard work to get there, but they also know it's worth it.

"So many people are eager to learn about sustainable gardening," says Marisa Thompson, urban horticulture specialist at New Mexico State University (NMSU). "All over the region, people attend classes to understand a little more about water usage, drought stress, soil health, beneficial insect populations (including pollinators), species selection and wildlife habitats."

Here are the most valuable lessons they learn.

Hot and Cold

The Challenge: In Phoenix, Arizona, summer high temperatures average over 100 degrees. But just 150 miles to the north in Flagstaff, the average winter lows are in the teens. Desert weather is harsh, and many gardeners in the Southwest have to contend with both scorching heat and frigid cold, along with scant rainfall even in the monsoon season that runs mid-June through September.

The Solution: Find the right plants for the right places. "Native and adapted plants that can tolerate our soils, arid environment and weather are a good way to maximize your landscape success and enjoyment," suggests retired horticulturist Curtis Smith on the NMSU Desert Blooms blog. Local county extension offices and native plant nurseries also offer invaluable recommendations for any garden, no matter what environment you plant in.

The Rewards: Southwestern natives produce flowers and foliage that rival their relatives around the country, and many have wonderful wildlife value. Native wildflowers and shrubs attract butterflies, hummingbirds and bees; even cacti support animals and birds like the cactus wren.

Dry as Dust

The Challenge: Albuquerque, New Mexico, and Atlanta, Georgia, both

This classic desert landscape features a concrete staircase with a mass planting of drought-tolerant echeveria on each side. A brugmansia tree is a focal point in the back.

experience hot summers and mild winters. But while Atlanta receives an average of 47 inches of rain a year, Albuquerque makes do with a paltry 9 inches, most of that in the summer monsoon season. Any time of year, water is a treasured commodity in the Southwest.

The Solution: It's super common for southwestern gardeners to use efficient, targeted irrigation like soaker hoses and micro sprayers. Water is too valuable (and expensive) to waste, so irrigation needs to get straight to the roots where it's needed. "Mulch is key!" Marisa says. "Mulching helps insulate plant roots and maintains soil moisture in both winter and summer. Not to mention, mulch makes a fantastic weed barrier."

The Rewards: Where the sun shines nearly every day, gardeners have plenty of time to enjoy the unique fruits of their labors. Plants that thrive there boast brilliant blooms and unique textures, all the more impressive contrasted with the parched landscapes around them.

Cantankerous Caliche

The Challenge: Ever sunk a shovel into the ground and heard the loud clang of impenetrable rock? Southwestern gardeners constantly contend with caliche (kuh-LEE-chay), a layer of soil that's been cemented together by calcium carbonate. It can be a thin crust or a layer several feet thick. The chance of striking caliche makes new plantings an adventure in the Southwest.

The Solution: Because caliche prevents plants from establishing healthy root systems and water from draining properly, southwestern gardeners have to punch through it. The planting hole should ideally be as deep as the root ball and four to five times as wide. "The goal is to get perennial roots to grow out horizontally in the soil where oxygen is available and water can be applied," Marisa says.

The Rewards: Desert gardening is tough, but not impossible. Resilient and charming plants support bountiful wildlife, including more hummingbird species than anywhere else in the States. Southwestern gardeners are thoughtful and dedicated stewards of their land, and are rewarded with spectacular gifts every day.

Sassy Summer Sunset yarrow tolerates drought yet offers clusters of fiery-hued blooms.

Drought Gardening Advice

Save water when your landscape is at its driest.

- Water only perennials and edibles; skip the annuals that can be replaced next year.

- Use targeted irrigation early or late in the day to lose less water to evaporation.

- Replace grass with more drought-friendly solutions.

- Save rainwater in a barrel or other container if it's allowed in your area.

- Add a heavy layer of mulch around plants to keep more moisture near the roots.

Male pyrrhuloxia
on guajillo tree

The Desert Dweller

Pyrrhuloxias make southern scrublands their year-round home on the range.

by Ken Keffer

"A beautiful family of pyrrhuloxias started visiting our apartment balcony in late March. They're so entertaining!"

Jim Lacoss
TUCSON, ARIZONA

Arizona hot spots

Whether you're local or planning a trip to southern Arizona, Saguaro National Park and Sabino Canyon Recreation Area are both wonderful places to search for pyrrhuloxias.

Open-air feeding

Entice pyrrhuloxias, and a wide variety of other birds, to stop in your backyard with a simple bamboo tray feeder such as this $30 feeder from *HomeDepot.com*.

THINK OF A **PYRRHULOXIA** as a southwestern cardinal. The name *pyrrhuloxia* combines the scientific terms for bullfinches and crossbills. Though not related to those species, the pyrrhuloxia has a very similar-looking bill. The bird is actually in the *Cardinalis* genus, with the more widespread and familiar northern cardinal.

The pyrrhuloxia is a favorite of Brad Brockman, a Wild Birds Unlimited store owner in Tucson, Arizona. "They have such an exotic look—almost parrotlike because of the shape of their beaks," he says.

A long, thin, wispy crest helps give the species a particularly whimsical look. The slate-gray birds have varying amounts of red in their plumage. In addition to the crimson highlights in the crests, wings and tails of female birds, males also show red in both their faces and bellies.

The species is a year-round resident in central Mexico and north into the southwestern United States from roughly Phoenix, Arizona, to Corpus Christi, Texas. It tends to prefer drier habitats like thorn scrub, mesquite and upland desert areas.

During the breeding season, male and female pyrrhuloxias create territories. Boundary lines are established with vocalizations reminiscent of a cardinal's pure repetitive whistle. Brad notes that the two species have a similar sound, but to his ear, pyrrhuloxia calls have a hollow and piercing quality to them.

Males still maintain boundaries after females settle in and build cup-shaped nests during the breeding season. Like cardinals, the female will sometimes sing from the nest while incubating a clutch of two to four eggs.

By late summer and into the winter, the aggressively defended territorial perimeters are loosened. Although some sources mention huge winter flocks of pyrrhuloxias, Brad has never encountered these congregations. Instead, he often sees small numbers of the species visiting backyard bird feeders.

Unsurprisingly, the feeding habitats of pyrrhuloxias mirror cardinals. Platforms, trays and ground feeding are all good options to allow these songbirds to feed.

Sunflower and safflower seeds are a traditional food choice, but the species eats a variety of things, according to Brad. "I have seen them stick their faces right into an orange," he says. A pyrrhuloxia will also take peanuts, mealworms and even jelly.

Natural food sources include seeds from grasses and shrubs, cactus fruit and various insects. Consider putting out a birdbath to provide drinking water and a place for them to take a quick dip in the desert heat.

Halfdan Lem
Rhododendron

Q. How do I protect plants, especially my rhododendrons, from heat waves?

Mary Anne Thygesen PORTLAND, OR

Melinda: Make sure the plants receive sufficient moisture before, during and after a heat wave. Water the soil in the evening, or in the early in the morning (between 2 a.m. and 6 a.m.) when it's still cooler and the plants are better able to absorb the water. Then watch for subtle signs that your plants might need water. Leaves will turn a somewhat blue- or gray-green color before wilting. This is the right time to give the plants some moisture. Even though wilted leaves may perk up after watering, some permanent damage may have occurred. If you haven't already, mulch the soil to help moderate the ground temperature and conserve moisture. You can also try to provide plants with some shade during extremely hot weather. Create a temporary structure that's set 18 inches above the top of the plant to protect it from the heat.

How do you beat the heat in your summer garden?

Readers share tried-and-true tips for staying cool and keeping plants healthy

With sunscreen on and a bottle of water nearby,
I work in the garden around 9 a.m. to avoid mosquitoes.
I begin with the sunny areas and move to shady ones as the
morning wears on. I finish no later than noon, often earlier.

Juli Seyfried CINCINNATI, OH

I use a **small adjustable umbrella** to protect me from
the direct sun.

Nancy Pedersen CENTER CITY, MN

I work in the **late afternoon** because it's light out until
9 p.m.

Cleone Benson Larson SALT LAKE CITY, UT

I water early in the morning so less water
evaporates throughout the day.

Jimmy Vicars PRINCETON, WV

Drought-tolerant plants are a must. We're
on a well, and the last thing we want is to
have it run dry because we're watering the
garden. Bee balm and coneflowers are ideal
for dry conditions.

Jen St. Louis ELMIRA, ON

Misters in the garden. Find the kind
designed for the end of a hose at any home
improvement store. They cool a large area
with subtle mist and provide water to thirsty
plants and insects.

Kathryn Rucci ORLANDO, FL

Nature Photography In the Rain

Don't let wet weather keep you from capturing great nature photography moments!

SUMMER IS THE WET SEASON in Florida. Nearly every day, we can expect at least some showers, and when a weather system parks itself over top of us, we may have more rain than sun for days on end. Rainy weather may slow down some wildlife, but for the most part, the natural world continues to go about its business. This can be a great time for nature photography, as long as you follow a few basic tips.

Protect your camera's lens.

Most cameras can stand a little moisture, but if your lens gets rain drops on it, you'll have to stop to clean it, which means you'll miss your shot. Use a lens hood on a higher-end camera, attach an umbrella to a tripod, or simply keep the front of the camera pointed down a bit and away from the wind.

Use your macro settings.

Raindrops on roses make for lovely nature photography shots. Emphasize the up-close beauty by using the macro setting on your camera, which allows you to capture detail.

Look for unusual shots.

Water droplets can magnify detail, and a sheet of rain can lend a filtered look to a shot. The best nature photography looks at usual subjects in unusual ways—use rainy weather as a chance to see the world a little bit differently.

Capture rainy day behavior.

Animals easily adjust their routines in rainy weather. Find butterflies taking shelter or get a few shots of the rain sliding off a duck's back (it really does happen).

When it snows in Maine, my backyard transforms into a white winter wonderland. Birds take advantage of my many feeders. I love watching them interact with each other or simply stop by to pay me a visit through my camera lens. This white-breasted nuthatch was very determined to get its fill from my feeder, even though the seeds were ice-coated from freezing rain. With the sun shining and that sharp little beak at work, it got its meal.

Catherine Melvin
WINDHAM, ME

I took this picture of a northern mockingbird at the San Antonio Botanical Garden. Some spring rain showers had started to move in, so I was preparing to leave when this mockingbird landed on a nearby railing. It was just getting ready to ruffle its feathers when I snapped the photo. I really liked its expression as it looked up at the sky while tiny raindrops fell around it.

Hannah Tripp
KING GEORGE, VA

A rainy day in Connecticut made this find extra special. As I walked among the dahlias, this brightly sunset colored one jumped out at me as it sat waiting for the sun to return.

Kimberly Sandberg
ENDERS ISLAND, CT

Staying Put
Unlike many other birds, northern cardinals don't migrate—they stay in the same place year-round.

This stunning male northern cardinal visited my feeder. If you look closely enough, you'll see some crumbs on his bill from the seeds he just ate. I have some health problems, so I don't get out much. I'm thankful for the birds that come to hang out in my yard.

Karen Sons CROWN POINT, IN

Summer Rain

"It just got done raining; I love the droplets on the tiger lilies. It was summer and I took the picture in my yard," says Kimberly Jo Wulfekuhle.

Finding Peace

"My mother used to grow beautiful roses, and one of her favorites was the Peace rose. When I was establishing my own garden, I couldn't find a Peace rose but came across this Golden Peace, which is almost identical. One summer it had spectacular blooms. This photo after a rain has always been one of my favorites," says Susan Terry.

Daylily Daydreams

"A few years ago, I was out on a summer morning photographing daylilies to enter in our local Daylily Club photo contest. I took this photo at Old Prairie Town Botanical Gardens in Topeka, Kansas, where I live. This variety is Treasure of the Southwest. I think it is unique because it has water droplets on the petals," says Mary Zeller.

Raindrops on Roses

"I love roses. I took this picture right after a summer rain," says Teresa Cipperly.

Swing Time
Hang perches, like a hummingbird swing, near sugar-water feeders for hummingbirds to rest.

One rainy afternoon in June, a female ruby-throat took a little break from buzzing around the flowers and feeders to perch on the hummingbird swing. She stayed there for some time, and it was fun to grab the camera and capture the moment. I love how fluffed and ruffled her feathers are from the rain.

Lauren Slack WATERVILLE, MN

Late-Season Stars

Both low-maintenance and a favorite with pollinators, colorful asters are ready for a leading role in your fall garden

by Wendy Helfenbaum

Make asters the focal point in an autumn floral bouquet.

COME FALL, a surge of vibrant color is welcome in most gardens.

Asters, true to their name's meaning of "star" in Greek, are proven performers, providing a gorgeous display of pink, purple, blue and white blossoms that perk up dreary beds. Some of these wildflowers are native to North America, and are readily available and easy to grow, making them a smart choice in any landscape.

Ranging from 1 to 6 feet tall and 1 to 4 feet wide, asters are popular because they are relatively free of problems and are also deer resistant, says Evan Santi, president of Urban Plantscapes, which services the Pittsburgh, Pennsylvania and New York City areas.

"They are related to sunflowers and chrysanthemums and have that same look if you examine the structure of the flower," Evan says.

Beyond offering gardeners stunning blooms, asters draw a flurry of wildlife to their symphony of color, says Evan.

Plenty of Variety

North American asters fall into the herbaceous perennial family *Asteraceae.* You will find a variety of asters available, including heath, calico, aromatic, smooth and wood,

A white-lined sphinx moth visiting Alma Potschke asters.

in addition to the two most popular aster species: New York and New England.

"I usually recommend people go with the natives because they're just beautiful," Evan says. "They offer pollen and nectar in very late fall and sometimes even early winter, which are lacking later in the season for the bees and other wildlife."

New York asters are hardy in Zones 4 to 8 while New England ones are hardy to Zones 3 to 8, and both produce clusters of star-shaped blossoms. Though quite similar, you can tell them apart: New York asters (*Symphyotrichum novi-belgii*) usually grow 2 to 3 feet tall and have thin stems and smooth leaves while New England asters (*S. novae-angliae*) reach 3 to 4 feet tall with thick stems, hairy leaves and denser flowers.

"New England is a bit more drought tolerant," Evan says, "and the New York aster is also called purple aster because of its iconic purple color."

He also recommends three other picks in particular: The blue wood aster (*S. cordifolium*) is a beautiful lavender bluish flower; the parasol whitetop or flat-topped white (*Doellingeria umbellata*) has unique-looking white petals; and the gorgeous aromatic aster (*S. oblongifolium*) is known for its aroma, which attracts all types of birds and bees.

Aster Care

Asters can be planted any time during the growing season, and most can tolerate a wide range of soil types.

"Native asters do not require a ton of fertilizer," Evan says. He recommends that you use the same kind of fertilizer that you would also use throughout the rest of your garden.

Established asters have to be watered only in extreme heat and drought, while the swamp aster (*S. puniceum*) excels in wet soil.

New England asters

New York asters

Purple Dome aster

Aromatic asters

Harrington's Pink asters

Blue wood asters

Asters prefer full sun, which helps them develop strong stems. Some varieties tolerate part shade but will produce fewer blooms. Planting in well-draining soil with good air circulation helps prevent powdery mildew and rust, which can affect some asters. Amend the soil each spring by spreading compost around the base of plants.

Top with mulch to retain moisture.

Asters growing over 3 feet tall may need staking at the beginning of the season so plants don't fall over, according to Evan. To get more blooms, pinch the tops of asters in late June, which will promote branching and create a shorter, bushier plant that extends the flowering season.

Alpine asters

Five to Try
Add a pop to the garden with these New England aster picks
- Alma Potschke
- Harrington's Pink
- Hella Lacy
- Purple Dome
- September Ruby

Though Evan points out that it can take time to do this because there are so many stems, "you'll get that big splash at the end," he says.

Showcase asters among other late-summer bloomers. Planted alongside daisies and daylilies, taller asters offer color well into late fall. Shorter ones shine near low-growing geraniums.

"I like the way asters look with Joe Pye weed, purple coneflower, blazing star, yarrow and goldenrod," Evan says. Tucked in front of ornamental grasses, asters provide a tiered effect, he adds.

Fall To-Do's

You don't need to do much to existing asters, since leaving them standing is helpful for the birds and other wildlife.

Many asters self-seed after blooming, so if you don't want seedlings popping up in unwanted places, trim off the spent flowers. You can propagate asters every three to four years if they become unruly and you want more plants.

"Some asters grow from rhizomes, so you can divide them in the off-season," Evan says.

He recommends lifting the plant and cutting off the outer sections, making sure to include several shoots and roots, and then transplanting them immediately.

Flat-topped white asters

Use a compostable bag when raking leaves, like this jute sack. They're better for the environment than plastic waste bags.

Good as Gold

Use fall leaves to improve soil, make free mulch and expand your garden beds

by Sally Roth

SHADE TREES provide plenty of benefits year-round: A cool spot to sit in summer, shelter and food for birds and insects in every season, beautiful colors in fall ... and then a blizzard of falling leaves.

Instead of bagging up autumn leaves and carting them to the curb, give them a new purpose. They're too valuable to discard. For starters, they're free mulch!

Use your lawn mower to chop them to bits, then bag them and dump that leaf confetti in your gardens. A 2-to-3-inch layer of chopped leaves makes your soil lighter and fluffier as it slowly decomposes, so plant roots grow better and weeds don't sprout.

If you have too many leaves for your garden to handle, rake them onto an old bedsheet, gather up the corners and pile them in a discreet corner of the yard. Even a massive heap sinks down quickly, and you'll be harvesting compost.

Thank the many decomposer critters that do the work—worms, snails, slugs, beetles, millipedes and isopods like sow bugs, all aided by fungal decomposition. As they break down and digest the leaves, the whole thing slowly turns into leaf mold, or humus, a dark, crumbly compost plants love.

A dense layer of leaves will kill lawn grass, but sometimes that's exactly what you want! To make a brand-new garden spot, try sheet mulching. First, dig a shallow trench around the bed and cut the grass short. Cover the area with brown cardboard or paper bags to block the light, wet it down, then top it with several inches of leaves. Soak the whole thing again so the leaves don't blow around.

Layers smother the turf while making the soil ripe for next year. Leave the grass-killing layers in place and dig the planting holes in the new bed. Growing in leaf compost is a little different than soil, so do some research about proper care before you plant.

Or keep the prettiest leaves for art projects. Glue a few colored ones to pumpkins, or use a white paint pen to draw on dry, pressed leaves. Frame a single leaf under glass as a trophy of your fall efforts.

Easy Breezy

Before you start up the mower or pick up a rake, let the wind do some work. Autumn winds blow leaves under hedges and shrubs and nestle them around perennials, insulating plant roots from winter cold and creating natural mulch as the leaves decay. Just make sure they don't pile up within 6 inches of trees' and shrubs' bases. As a bonus, thrashers, native sparrows, robins, towhees and others sort through the leaves to feast on insects and other tidbits.

Create a Fall Focal Point

Add a creative highlight to any outdoor area with these container garden ideas

by Luke Miller

WHEN SUMMER STARTS TO **FADE** and cooler temperatures prevail, it's time to jazz up your outdoor living space with fresh fall decor in a pot.

Rather than simply placing a potted plant by the doorway, use this season to unleash your inner artist and create a stunning fall vignette.

Autumn Display

For a wonderfully easy and quick container creation, try pairing up assorted mums and chartreuse sweet potato vine (*Ipomoea batatas*) to serve as the focal point. Then place squash, pumpkins and gourds around the container to complete the fall picture.

Go for Grass

Ornamental grasses are a popular fall container plant, since they often peak during the season with ripening flower heads and changing foliage. Purple fountain grass goes perfectly in containers, working with other plants or calling attention to itself without any help.

Mum's the Word

Chrysanthemums are the most recognizable fall flower and for good reason—they stand out! They're bold enough to work on their own, but they also look great in combination with complementary colors.

All Hail Kale!

Kale grows in popularity year after year. Edible varieties are valued for their nutrients, while ornamental varieties, called flowering kale, are a visual delight in the autumn garden. They are frost tolerant and look more colorful as temperatures drop. Flowering kale plants are also more compact than edible varieties.

Keep it Simple

If you don't want to make a lot of fuss creating a display, stick with one plant and put it in a key location where it's easily seen and enjoyed. Gerbera daisies are an unexpected delight, blooming in a range of colors right until frost. Orange is a traditional fall color, but there are whites, yellows and pinks too.

A Pumpkin Plan

Nothing says fall quite like a pumpkin, which coincidentally can be turned into a simply perfect planter. It's sure to bring on some smiles! Plant directly inside the pumpkin after drilling a few drainage holes, or just drop a pot into the gourd, creating a fun and festive container for flowers.

1. Purple fountain grass and Fire Light panicle hydrangea
2. Lemon Coral sedum, polka dot plant, mini pumpkins and purple fountain grass
3. Ornamental kale, a leafy spiller and ornamental grass
4. Carved-out pumpkin with chrysanthemums
5. Chrysanthemums, red cabbage and tapestry vine

Black-capped chickadees are leaders of the winter flocks.

Mixed Winter Flocks

Discover why some birds travel in mixed-species flocks and find out how to watch this behavior for yourself

by Kenn and Kimberly Kaufman

Northern cardinals, a tufted titmouse and a black-capped chickadee share a feeder.

Black-capped chickadees

These busy, acrobatic little birds live in pairs or family groups during the summer, but in winter they gather in groups of of a dozen or more.

Dark-eyed junco

IT'S NOT UNCOMMON FOR STILL, silent winter landscapes to be suddenly disrupted by distant birdcalls. Within moments, half a dozen kinds of birds appear, flitting among tree branches, climbing up trunks, hanging upside down from twigs. For just a few minutes, the birds bring life to the area with colors, sounds and movement. Then they all fly away together. These mixed flocks of birds are one of winter's special features. If you're aware of the activity, you may be able to observe them practically anywhere in North America, and possibly in your own backyard.

Safety in Numbers

So why do we see these mixed flocks? It's probably not just because birds enjoy one another's company. For many, there's a good reason for flocking: It's safer than traveling alone. Searching for food out in the wild takes lots of concentration, and it's hard to look for seeds or berries and watch for danger at the same time. With more birds in the flock, there's a better chance that a swooping hawk or prowling cat will be spotted while there's still time to sound the alarm and make a getaway.

Leaders of the Pack

When you see a mixed flock moving through the trees, it may seem as if they're all acting independently. But there are definite leaders and followers.

In treetop flocks, the leaders are usually chickadees. These busy, acrobatic little birds live in pairs or family groups during the summer, but in winter they gather in groups of a dozen or more. These flocks stick together throughout the cold months. As they make a regular circuit through the woods, other small birds fall in with them, following the lead of the chickadees—nuthatches, brown creepers, titmice, kinglets, downy woodpeckers and yellow-rumped warblers among them. These birds are clued in to the voices of their chickadee leaders, and when they hear an alarm note, they immediately look around for danger.

North America has several species of chickadees in different regions—including black-capped chickadees across the Northern states and Canada, Carolina chickadees in the Southeast, mountain chickadees in the Rockies

White-breasted nuthatch

and chestnut-backed chickadees in the Pacific Northwest—but they all serve as flock leaders in their own areas.

Zone Defense

Active and alert, chickadees may be quicker to spot danger than the other birds that flock with them. For example, brown creepers, creeping up trees with their faces close to the bark, can't be scanning in all directions as easily as a chickadee can.

The followers may not help the chickadees much, but they don't do any harm either. They usually aren't competing for the same food, since they all seek nutrition in different ways. Woodpeckers, nuthatches and creepers examine the bark of trunks and large limbs, with the nuthatches often going down trees headfirst. Kinglets may hover under the tips of twigs, while titmice often hang upside down from heavier branches. So several kinds of birds can forage in the same tree without any direct competition.

It might seem as if the same birds are traveling with the chickadees all day, but that isn't necessarily so. Some of these birds have their own winter territories, and they'll stay with the flock only while it travels through their own corner of the woods. A white-breasted nuthatch, for instance, will follow right along with the chickadees until they come to the edge of its territory—then it will drop out, and another nuthatch from the neighboring territory will take its place in the flock.

Flocks at the Feeder

These winter flocks like to keep moving. Instinct tells them to travel within their home range so that they don't use up all the food in any one spot. So even if you have a backyard filled with bountiful bird feeders, a flock is likely to arrive, stay for a short while and then move on. Don't worry, though: It will be back, perhaps several times a day.

Pine siskins and
American goldfinches

Male and female northern cardinals

4 Tips to Attract Mixed Flocks This Winter

Provide cover. Birds seek protection from predators and from extreme weather. Pine, cedar and spruce are great options in all seasons, but especially in winter. Winter visitors will also greatly appreciate brush piles you can easily make out of fallen limbs and branches.

Serve good eats. Black-oil sunflower seed, peanuts and suet provide important nutrients in winter. For some birds in mixed flocks, berries are also important. Some of our backyard favorites are serviceberry, dogwood, juniper, wild grape and viburnum.

Put out ground feeders. Some winter flocks include juncos and native sparrows, which prefer to forage on or near the ground. A low tray-style feeder is best, but in a pinch you can sprinkle seed directly on the ground or on packed snow.

Add fresh water. In areas with wintry weather, open water can be hard to find. Winter flocks are much more likely to visit a backyard with fresh water. Keep the water clean, and think about adding a birdbath heater.

Treetop flocks led by chickadees represent only one kind of mixed winter flock. There are also mixed flocks of seed-eating birds that live close to the ground, often including dark-eyed juncos, American tree sparrows, white-throated sparrows, white-crowned sparrows and others. Another type of winter flock may include goldfinches, pine siskins and redpolls.

Keep an eye out for these winter flocks, either out in the woods or among the birds that visit your yard. When you spot one of these mixed gatherings, watch to see how the different species interact, and see if you can figure out which birds are the leaders and which are the followers. You'll find that these diverse flocks add variety and excitement to your winter birding.

Winter Garden Flair

When the snow falls, these plants still shine

by Jodi Helmer

❮ Snowdrop

GALANTHUS NIVALIS,
ZONES 3 TO 8

These 4-to-6-inch-tall perennials thrive in cool climates. The early-blooming bulbs produce delicate white flowers and the thin, dark green leaves disappear when the bulbs go dormant. Plant snowdrop bulbs at least 2 inches deep in groups during fall. Snowdrops can self-seed, so give them plenty of space to spread.

Why we love it: Falling snow and cold winters won't stop snowdrops from pushing through the soil.

⌃ Christmas rose

HELLEBORUS NIGER,
ZONES 3 TO 8

Christmas rose, also known as black hellebore, takes a long time to establish but is worth the wait. It blooms in winter in warm areas and does best in part to full shade. A sheltered location with protection from cold winds will keep the deeply lobed, dark green leaves looking good all winter long.

Why we love it: In regions with warmer winters, Christmas rose produces large white flowers with yellow stamens in December.

⌃ Buttercup winterhazel

CORYLOPSIS PAUCIFLORA, ZONES 6 TO 8

Buttercup winterhazel earned its name thanks to its abundant, mildly fragrant yellow flowers that appear in late winter or spring. It has light green leaves that turn yellow or chartreuse in the fall. Grow in acidic, moist, well-draining soil and full sun to part shade.

Why we love it: Neatly compact at 4 to 6 feet tall and wide, it's ideal for smaller gardens.

❮ Winter jasmine

JASMINUM NUDIFLORUM, ZONES 6 TO 10

Given its tolerance of drought, shade, pests and diseases, winter jasmine is a great choice for challenging conditions. The semievergreen shrub stands around 5 feet tall, but its vines stretch up to 15 feet. Flowers appear in late winter to early spring.

Why we love it: The shrub's long vines can be trained with a trellis to create a screen or grown as a ground cover on slopes and banks.

⌃ Switchgrass

PANICUM VIRGATUM, ZONES 3 TO 10

When it comes to low-maintenance grasses, switchgrass is a winner. This native option grows best in full sun and moist soil, a top pick for rain gardens. Flower spikes rise a foot or two above the grass and produce light pink blooms in mid- to late summer. It can be aggressive, so consider a cultivar that spreads less.

Why we love it: The seeds last into the winter, providing a food source for hungry birds.

⌃ Red Twig Dogwood

CORNUS SERICEA,
ZONES 2 TO 7

Reaching 6 to 9 feet tall and spreading up to 10 feet wide, red twig dogwood can't be missed. Butterflies visit its white flowers in late spring. The blooms then turn into white fruit, attracting birds. This shrub prefers full sun to part shade and medium to wet soil.

Why we love it: Look for bright red stems in barren landscapes; the youngest offer the most vibrant color.

⌃ Springwood Pink Winter Heath

ERICA CARNEA, ZONES 5 TO 7

Choose this compact evergreen plant for garden interest in all four seasons. Also known as snow heath, it prefers acidic soil and full sun to part shade. The slow-growing ground cover is native to the Alps in Europe. Look for needlelike green foliage with bronze tips.

Why we love it: Pink-tinted blooms appear from January to March, adding subtle color to the landscape.

❯ Northern Sea Oats

CHASMANTHIUM LATIFOLIUM,
ZONES 4 TO 9

Northern sea oats is a native ornamental grass that tolerates shade. The seed heads start out green in spring before transitioning to a purplish bronze over the summer. The plant can spread aggressively, so give it room in moist soil. Several skipper butterflies use this grass as a host plant.

Why we love it: By winter, the foliage turns a copper tone.

❯ Winterberry

ILEX VERTICILLATA,
ZONES 3 TO 9

This deciduous holly has dark green leaves that fade to gold or maroon in the fall. The shrub grows well in full sun to part shade and wet soil. One male plant can pollinate up to five female, berry-producing plants.
Why we love it: As the name implies, bright red berries appear after the first frost.

❮ Winter daphne

DAPHNE ODORA, ZONES 7 TO 9

When planted in part shade and moist, well-draining soil, winter daphne thrives in warmer climates and delights gardeners with bright, rosy blooms. It can also be kept in containers and overwintered inside.
Why we love it: The shrub's fragrant flowers, in shades from light pink to reddish purple, bloom between January and April.

CHAPTER 5

Go Big!

Some say go big or go home, but at *Birds & Blooms*, we say go big and *stay* home! Plant bigger blooms, attract larger birds and give small spaces a huge impact. Learn how here.

Larger than Life

In nature, you sometimes have to look long and hard to see the hidden beauty around you. But that's not the case here!

Large and in Charge

Sunflowers (left) are some of the largest flowers that you can grow in your backyard. Just about any sunflower would make a statement, but the mammoth varieties lead the pack, growing more than 10 feet tall! Similarly, there's a reason the plant shown here has earned the name elephant's ears. Some of the leaf blades grow 3 to 4 feet long. Below: The cecropia is the largest moth in North America.

Eye Illusions

Scissor-tailed flycatchers (top) get half of their size from their long tails. Above, an American white pelican has an impressive 108-inch wingspan. And the giant swallowtail (left) takes the honor as the largest North American butterfly, with a wingspan up to 6 inches.

Tropical Feel
Hibiscus flowers can grow up to dinner-plate size (8 to 10 inches) and give a "touch of the tropics" to backyards across North America.

Nature's Greats
The great gray owl is by far the largest owl in North America at 27 inches long. The next closest is the snowy owl at a mere 23 inches. The great gray has a wingspan of 52 inches.

Have a Nice Day

Above, this flower bed planted with yellow ornamental peppers and iresine at Cantigny Gardens in Wheaton, Illinois, can't help but make you smile. At left, the dahlia is another flower that can make a big impact in your garden. Look for plants classified as giant dahlias if you want blooms more than 10 inches in diameter. Below, the praying mantis might seem like a small backyard visitor, but it can grow several inches long, making it one of the most visible insects in the garden.

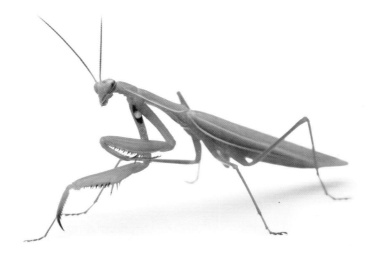

Moth Tales

Readers share cool snapshots of these mysterious fliers

Each year, I try to show my young grandson something new in nature. One day we were blessed to find this rarely seen example of a North American giant silk moth: a polyphemus! This beautiful male was ready to go a-courtin'. Adults have no mouths to eat with, so they have less than two weeks to find a mate and set the next generation on its journey.

Tim Bosley
SOUTH LYON, MI

I took this photo at Beulah Baptist Church in Muscadine, Alabama. I was walking to my Sunday school class and noticed it sitting on the railing between the classrooms. After some research I found that she is a citheronia regalis.

Stephanie Perry, MUSCADINE, AL

I found this cecropia moth on the side of my potting bench. It was around for only about a week, and it likely left after mating. I have never seen one before or since.

Calvin Anderson
PEABODY, MA

When a butterfly chooses your garden, it's magical. Your cares fade away with each flap of their wings. I grow several flowering plants to attract these beauties. In particular, this zebra longwing needs its host plant, passionflower, for its caterpillars to munch on. As adults, the species enjoys the bright red blossoms of jatropha shrubs and this yellow starry rosinweed.

Doreen Damm
NEW PORT RICHEY, FL

For 44 years I have lived in Minnesota and I had never seen a luna moth before. I was doing some work when this one buzzed my head and landed about 10 feet away, as if begging me to take its picture. I was more than happy to oblige.

Jason Nibbe
LAKE CITY, MN

The color contrast in this photo is pretty intense. I love how the bold black swallowtail rested with its wings open on the pink clematis bloom. This butterfly felt special to me because it was one of the first I spotted that spring.

Linda Carissimi
SIMSBURY, CT

Alabama's largest butterfly is the giant swallowtail, with a wingspan of up to 7 inches. I used my Nikon D3300 DSLR camera to capture this shot of a female laying eggs on a citrus tree leaf in my front yard. Giant swallowtails visit the zinnias in my garden almost daily.

Amos Tindell ENTERPRISE, AL

Garden Giants

Grow the biggest blooms on the block

by Kirsten Schrader

❰ Globemaster Allium

ALLIUM, ZONES 4 TO 9

Add major drama to your garden with 8-to-10-inch purple globes. Flower heads burst to life in late spring, featuring densely packed florets that make up the mega blooms.

Why we love it: They're tall too! Growing 3 to 4 feet high, these alliums command attention in a landscape.

❱ Incrediball Hydrangea

HYDRANGEA ARBORESCENS, ZONES 3 TO 9

Sturdy stems support massive summer-blooming white flowers. The nearly 12-inch blooms begin green, mature to white and then fade back to green later in the season. To encourage new growth and flowering, prune this shrub in late winter.

Why we love it: Unlike other large hydrangeas, Incrediball won't flop over, even after a strong rain.

❰ California Giants zinnia

ZINNIA ELEGANS, ANNUAL

Brighten up your backyard with long-lasting, colorful zinnias. Plant a package of seeds in full sun, and soon a rainbow of colors emerges. These heirloom seeds were developed around the 1920s and still delight gardeners today.

Why we love it: Stems may reach 4 feet tall, and the semi-double blooms are 5 inches across. Harvest these giants as cut flowers to add an explosion of color to your kitchen counter.

❰ Thomas Edison Dinnerplate Dahlia

DAHLIA, ZONES 8 TO 11

Make some room at the back of a sunny garden bed for this 3-to-4-foot purple stunner. The Thomas Edison variety was first introduced in 1929 and remains one of the best purple dahlias on the market. In places where dahlias aren't hardy, bring the tuberous roots indoors for the winter and replant in spring.

Why we love it: Dahlias are ideal cut flowers. Display the jumbo 8-inch blooms in vases all over your home.

‹ Bigleaf Magnolia

MAGNOLIA MACROPHYLLA, ZONES 5 TO 8

Although this magnolia is considered a medium-size tree, it has the largest leaves and flowers of any North American deciduous species.

Why we love it: Take a sniff! Fragrant white flowers are 8 to 12 inches across and pop in summer. An up-close look reveals beautiful purple centers.

⌃ Pikes Peak Sunflower

HELIANTHUS, ANNUAL

Give these giants a sunny spot and some room to grow. Fourteen-inch flower heads reach for the sun atop stately stalks as high as 15 feet.

Why we love it: Big seeds mean big plants. This variety produces the largest sunflower seeds in the world. Birds might beat you to the seed harvest, though.

› Diva's Choice Daylily

HEMEROCALLIS, ZONES 3 TO 9

This diva demands attention. Give it a prime spot in your perennial or container garden, and let the 6-inch fragrant flowers shine. With a grand appearance in early summer, the flowers repeat throughout the summer and the fall.

Why we love it: Not only is this pink starlet a big bloomer, it provides interest. From the scalloped yellow trim to the green centers, there's so much to see. Plus, hummingbirds and butterflies can't resist the long-lived nectar source.

❮ Double White Angel's Trumpet

BRUGMANSIA X CANDIDA,
ZONES 8 TO 10

☀ ☁ ⛅

Grab a chair and settle in next to this angel's trumpet each evening. The sweet fragrance from just one plant is enough to perfume the whole backyard. Pick a sunny spot for the shrub, and plant it in well-drained soil. Beware: All parts of angel's trumpet are harmful to humans and pets.

Why we love it: By early fall, as many as 100 ruffled double blooms dangle from stems covered with tobacco-like foliage. Plus, the 10-inch flowers are deer-resistant.

❮ Summer Storm Hibiscus

HIBISCUS, ZONES 4 TO 9

☀ ☁ ⛅

It's compact for a hibiscus at only about 4 feet tall, but the small size doesn't affect the showy pink flowers. The 8-to-10-inch flowers wow until fall, when the leaves turn yellow-orange. Plant Summer Storm in full sun and be on the lookout for hummingbird visitors.

Why we love it: Peel your eyes away from the gigantic blossoms and take notice of the beautiful, dark purple foliage.

❯ The President Clematis

CLEMATIS, ZONES 4 TO 8

☀ ☁ ⛅

Find a bare fence, trellis or post and let this climber do its thing. Purple flowers as big as 8 inches flourish in May and June and then again in September and October. Hummingbirds might stop for a sweet treat during fall migration.

Why we love it: The show doesn't stop when the bold blooms fade—the seed heads are attractive even during the autumn months.

A Dozen Ways to Dazzle

Take your garden to the next level and make a huge impact with these easy ideas

by Rachael Liska

E ACH GARDEN, like the person who planted it, has its own personality. Wild. Romantic. Eccentric. Classy. But the one thing a garden shouldn't be known for is having a wallflower personality. Garner your garden the attention it deserves with these 12 tips and tricks.

1. Love the "Less is More" Rule.

It doesn't take much to make a statement, especially in a small garden. A single specimen tree, a brightly painted obelisk, a piece of stone sculpture—set out simple touches like these in highly visible or high-traffic areas.

2. Embrace Shapes.

Formally sculpted evergreens, the spiky fronds of a yucca or the striking ball of blooms atop an allium are good examples of how shapes can create intriguing focal points. Plant in groupings to make a statement or plot out points around the garden to help visually lead an observer's eye through the space.

3. Wow with Water.

There's something about the sound and appearance of water that speak to the human soul. Whether it's a quiet corner pond teeming with koi or a bubbling stone fountain among the roses, water is a strong element that can't be overlooked. For the biggest splash, opt for flowing water, such as waterfalls and streams. If space or budget is an issue, try smaller items like rain chains or a tabletop waterfall.

Find flowers with interesting shapes (like these alliums) to make a statement in your garden.

Seating creates a welcoming space.

Repurpose a fountain into a bold planter.

4. Offer a Seat.

A garden is lovely to look upon, but adding a bench invites visitors to sit down and soak in its beauty. A small seating area fitted with a couple of chairs and a bistro table is all you need to create an outdoor room. Set the space apart from its surroundings with a floor made from pavement, crushed stone or manicured grass. Go a step further by creating living walls with a few large shrubs.

5. Learn to Accessorize.

Instead of smaller elements competing for a viewer's attention, use the right garden accessories to spin harmony out of havoc. It's easy to achieve garden unity with structural elements, like large urns or gazing balls. (Here's your chance to go really big!) Try spacing identical pieces along a pathway or placing them in low-growing beds.

6. Catch a Drift.

Planting in drifts, or swaths of colors or textures, is easier said than done. It requires dedicating large areas to one kind of plant, but the attention-grabbing effect it can have on your garden is worth the work. Mass planting works well alongside pathways and garden bed borders. Good plant candidates include Russian sage, purple coneflower, Moonbeam coreopsis, Autumn Joy sedum, coral bells and ornamental grasses.

7. Master the Art of Unpredictability.

Every corner of your garden is an opportunity to show off your unique sense of style. A wall of planted garden boots or tea kettles will stop passersby in their tracks. Try grouping quirky collectibles together. Adorn a single tree with pretty beads and ornaments, hang a salvaged chandelier from a rustic arched arbor, or make a wine bottle tree.

8. Go Big.

Plant a few "garden peacocks"—plants with showy blooms or larger-than-life foliage—and get ready for the "oohs" and "aahs." Best bets? Delphinium for its gorgeous spikes of bountiful blossoms, canna for its bright blooms and tropical-like foliage, hydrangea for its impressive size, and blue hosta for its cool-hued leaves.

9. Create Layers.

Like a good outfit, layering builds interest, but it's important to mix textures and keep the color scheme harmonious. If you're not sure where to start, try planting a screen of dark evergreens, ornamental grass or dense shrubbery of the same variety. In front of that, add a row of plants with contrasting textures that require the same growing conditions. A low-growing bloomer—carpet roses, Walker's Low catmint or dianthus—along the outside border finishes the look.

Water always livens up the backyard.

10. Take a Walk.

Give your garden room to breathe by incorporating a bit of green space. Wide pathways, grassy courtyards, natural meadows and labyrinths generate an open-air feel. Plus, showier plants really shine when edging an unassuming strip of space.

11. Be Bold with Containers.

Magically make over any space with containers and the miniature gardens they hold. Think oversized—urns, tall stainless steel planters and upcycled wheelbarrows. Think colorful—glazed ceramic beauties in cobalt blue, sunset orange and lemon yellow finishes. Think dramatic—plants like red cordyline, angel's trumpet, hibiscus or flowering kale. How you display your container creations can be even more impactful than what is inside them. Secure your containers to a wall, hang them from a fence or stack them on a ladder.

12. Light Up the Night.

Well-placed lighting accentuates our most attractive attributes, and the same holds true for your garden. There are many options available when it comes to outdoor lighting, from pathway and accent lighting to deck and pond lights. Spotlight landscape features, like trees and plants with interesting foliage, and your garden will look as dapper in the dark as it does in the daytime.

Plant in large patches to really turn heads.

It always amazes me how colorful and large the blooms are on our garden's dahlia plants. My wife grows them in our backyard. I took this photo in the summer one year with a Canon 7D body and a Canon 70-200mm lens.

Jim Leonard
SALEM, OR

Backyard Birding in Small Spaces

Even if you have just 100 square feet, you can attract birds. Learn how to use the space to provide them food, water and shelter, and your feathered friends will visit.

by Ken Keffer

MARK TURNER

Garden for Birds
Planting a garden, even in containers, provides shelter and food. Goldfinches (shown here) are among the birds you can attract with plants.

Maximize Space with a Variety of Food and Feeders

Be patient when you first put out a feeder. It can take the birds quite a while before they feel comfortable around a new one. After the first birds start using it, others will be quick to take notice.

There are endless varieties of birdseed out there, but start with the basics when you have limited space. Thistle is an especially popular seed for American goldfinches, pine siskins and redpolls, with the bonus of being less attractive to squirrels. A thistle (Nyjer) tube feeder is a great choice for a small backyard.

Black oil sunflower seed is the pizza of bird food: Nearly everyone in the backyard will enjoy it. You can offer other quality seeds like safflower or even peanuts to satisfy other birds.

Another way to enhance your backyard is to offer different styles of bird feeders. While many species will readily perch at tube feeders, others will prefer a larger platform to sit on. You can hang feeders almost anywhere; try a hook that hangs from the branch of a tree. Mount feeders along a porch railing. You can also plant an arch in the ground and make your own feeding station.

Common redpolls don't mind sharing one feeder.

Food for Thought
Birds can spend up to 18 hours a day searching for food, so putting out a feeder really does help!

PHOTOGRAPHER: EMIKO FRANZEN. SET STYLIST: EMIKO FRANZEN. BUILDER: SAMUEL ROSENMAYER

Resist the urge to place a feeder in the center of your backyard, where the birds will have no shelter. Instead, put up multiple feeders in opposite corners of the yard. Or try moving a feeder closer to your house.

One Birdbath Can Do Wonders

Water can be even more effective than food in luring birds close. From the simple to the most decorative, there are countless birdbath styles available. Or you can craft your own out of almost anything.

Be sure to change your water every day. It can get dirty surprisingly quickly. Also, stagnant water can be a breeding pool for mosquitoes and other insects. You should give the birdbath a good scrubbing on occasion as well.

Fountains, spinners or misters are a nice touch; the movement can help attract more birds. It's worth adding a couple of rocks to your birdbath too. Beyond keeping the bath securely in place, they'll give the birds a better perch to drink or bathe from. Remember that most birds don't want water that is too deep. A couple of inches is plenty.

Consider a variety of feeders to attract a variety of birds.

Eastern towhees are ground feeders, but they will occasionally visit platform feeders for seed.

Keep it cool. Birds get hot too!

In the heat of summer, place your bath in the shade, if possible, and change the water frequently.

Birds like American robins need only about 2 inches of water in birdbaths.

In winter you can add a birdbath heater. Some of these perform better than others, so check for reviews. Some of the most effective heaters are built right into the birdbath. There are also separate heaters that sit in most any tray. Remember that glass birdbaths should be brought in for the winter.

Small Plants Do Double Duty

It's easy to overlook the importance of shelter to backyard birds. Sure, we all know birds need places to nest, but having some backyard plant cover can attract even more birds to your space all year.

Giving birds an easy place to retreat to helps protect them from predators. Some people retire the holiday tree to the backyard so it can provide shelter year round. Sprinkling some cracked corn or sunflower seed near the shelter might help entice species like thrashers, towhees and juncos. These birds rarely come to more traditional feeders but feel right at home feeding on the ground near cover.

Consider planting a native berry producer. With a berry-producing tree or shrub, you'll offer both protection and a bonus food source. Many shrubs provide good cover for birds.

Even a container shrub will help. Don't be surprised if a wren finds it a suitable place to build a nest. You can also put up a platform for robins or phoebes to use.

Especially with small backyards, it's important to remember that your space is just a part of the bird's home range. But with a little imagination, you can make the tiniest of yards an ideal habitat.

No Backyard? No Problem!

Even if you live in an apartment building or simply don't have a yard, you can still enjoy the birds. You'll be relying on surrounding habitats, but with careful observation, you can spot birds. Here's how:

Window feeders. There are feeders you can put right on your windows with suction cups. I use a suction cup suet feeder to get close-up looks at chickadees, nuthatches and woodpeckers.

Hanging basket. Try displaying some hummingbird-friendly flowers. In addition to hummers, you could also attract beautiful butterflies and maybe even a sphinx moth.

Invest in optics. I can easily see migrating warblers in the treetops from my apartment window. I also watch flocks of ducks, geese, gulls and even swans flying along Lake Michigan.

Look to the sky. If you live in a high-rise building, your best bet is to look up for flying birds and not down toward the feeders. Peregrine falcons and red-tailed hawks patrol the skies in many urban areas, so keep your eyes to the sky.

Focus on migration. It's always exciting to host new visitors. Spring and fall migration offer the best chances of something unexpected showing up in your area.

Pull in Pileateds

Attract this stunning woodpecker with the right feeder and a tree-filled yard

by Kelsey Roseth

PILEATED **WOODPECKERS** are big, bold and beautiful, sporting expansive white underwings, a flaming red crest, and black and white stripes on the face and neck. Males show off an extra pop of red on each cheek known as a "mustache mark."

Substantial Size

This 16-to-19-inch-long bird is believed to be the largest woodpecker in North America; the only larger species, the ivory-billed woodpecker, is suspected to be extinct.

Flight in Focus

When in the air, the species "has this distinctive undulating flight where they flap, flap, flap, then drop," says Keith Barker, a bird researcher and curator of genetic resources at the Bell Museum of Natural History at the University of Minnesota. "If you see something basically as big as a crow but flying that way, then it's this woodpecker."

Foraging for Grubs

At home in mature forests, pileated woodpeckers thrive when surrounded by dead trees and downed logs. They're known for drilling large rectangular holes into tree trunks and thick branches as they search for wood-boring beetle larvae, carpenter ants, termites and more.

Once carved, the holes offer shelter to owls, swifts, ducks, bats and pine martens. To attract pileateds, set out suet, a high-calorie snack, in a feeder that's large enough for the big birds.

Breeding Behavior

Male pileated woodpeckers kick off their courtships with dances that include bowing, scraping and stepping sideways in a circle around potential mates. When paired, they typically bond for life.

Attract a breeding duo by leaving dead trees standing or by securing a substantially sized nest box to a living tree.

Whether you buy a box online or build your own, just make sure it's 24 inches deep and about 1 foot wide and tall, with a 4-inch entry hole, and hang it 15 to 20 feet aboveground.

Help Their Habitat

Pileated woodpeckers are spotted year-round throughout the eastern half of the United States and along the West Coast.

"We often associate their decline with old-growth forests being cut down, which they are

Male pileated woodpecker

"Usually they're very skittish, but this pileated paid me no mind as he worked hard for his breakfast."

TJ Waller
GENEVA, FL

Powerful Sound
Pileated woodpeckers produce *cuk, cuk* or *wuk, wuk* sounds and a long series of high, clear piping calls. If one is nearby, you'll know it.

Good News
Although pileated populations declined in the past, the North American Breeding Bird Survey found a steady increase between 1966 and 2014.

very dependent on," says Sushma Reddy, curator of birds at the Bell Museum of Natural History.

"If there's a wooded area where people can leave dead branches on the ground, this supports biodiversity and may help to attract more birds."

In It to Win It

Bird-watchers turn their love of the hobby into thousands of dollars for conservation

by Kirsten Schrader

Big-Day Sighting
During the World Series of Birding, a rare (for New Jersey) painted bunting was spotted by Tony Croasdale and his team.

IMAGINE GOING ON A 24-HOUR bird-watching adventure. No sleep, meals on the run, even birding in the dark. Sounds fun, right? These daylong events are not only exciting, they directly benefit birds, the real winners in the world of competitive birding. Sure, there are winning teams and some participants get high honors for their fundraising efforts, but it's always the birds that come out on top.

Bird-watching competitions all over the country are major fundraisers for bird research and conservation. Most of the events use a version of the big-day concept (a race to see more species in 24 hours than your competitors). The rules and birding categories can vary, but there are two common goals among all the tournaments: raise as much money as possible for the birds, and have a lot of fun doing it.

Here are three events that are already making a huge impact and continue to grow and raise more and more money each year.

Great Texas Birding Classic

After enjoying more than 20 years of fun, the Great Texas Birding Classic (*birdingclassic.org*) is now more successful than ever. Shelly Plante, event organizer since 1999, says the competition has seen a huge boost in participation since 2013, when it opened up to include the entire state and not just the coastal regions.

Registration fees are now lower ($30-$50 for adults), and new categories, which include options

Young Birders
Shelly Plante of the Great Texas Birding Classic says kids get an appreciation for conservation by participating. Plus, they can spot special Texas birds, like the great kiskadee, above.

Night Birding

An American pelican was in northern Indiana when Rob Ripma did his big day during the Amos Butler Audubon Birdathon. He remembers going to look for the bird in the dark and having to use a spotlight to see it.

for regional, statewide and weeklong birding, attract more birders.

"The categories appeal to the hard-core birders, but beginners also have a place," Shelly says. "Some people come back to try to defend their title. Some try different tournaments. One family uses the event as the family trip."

The Great Texas Birding Classic lasts an entire month, April 15 to May 15. Teams choose their

Look Up!

This team, called Dallas ZOOM, participated in the Texas competition.

competition day, which gives them time to plan.

"When we went statewide, we tried to figure out a timing that would allow each team to take advantage of its own region," Shelly says. "Teams register by April 1 and then tell me their day within 24 hours of going out."

Winning teams work with Birding Classic staff to choose the grant projects they'd like to support. Previous grants have gone to creating accessible walking paths and bird-viewing areas at important refuges and state parks.

World Series of Birding

New Jersey Audubon's World Series of Birding (*worldseriesofbirding.org*) has a very unique characteristic—each team pays the registration fee (which goes to New Jersey Audubon), but then raises money, either through sponsors or pledges, for the nonprofit of *the team's* choice.

Founded in 1984 by legendary birder Pete Dunne, the World Series of Birding sets the standard for big-day fundraisers. While it follows the typical structure of 24 hours of birding, it features unique, challenging categories. For example, the Swarovski Carbon Footprint Challenge award goes to the team with the highest species count that also went green and didn't use any fossil fuel to get around.

CLOCKWISE FROM TOP LEFT: TOM VEZO/MINDEN; KARA BENSON, GREAT TEXAS BIRDING CLASSIC, TPWD (2)

Green Team

David Benson, Wes Homoya, Maggie Jaicamo and Chuck Benson were the Carbon Neutral team and did their big day for the Amos Butler Audubon Birdathon by bike.

David La Puma, director of New Jersey Audubon's Cape May Bird Observatory, has participated in the carbon footprint challenge; he and his teammates used bikes as their mode of transportation.

"We're constantly evolving the event, and a lot of things are changing," David says. "It's a great opportunity for organizations to come out here and compete. New Jersey is really one of the *birdiest* places in North America."

Cumulatively, the competition reaches an impressive 260 species. The New Jersey tournament had 80 teams in 2015 and is always looking to expand. The next World Series is on May 14.

Amos Butler Audubon Birdathon

As the premier fundraising event for the Amos Butler Audubon (*amosbutleraudubon.org*) in central Indiana, the annual Birdathon raised almost $39,000 in 2015. That money funded a record 10 grants for projects like protecting the wintering territory of cerulean warblers, research on native birds and local habitat restoration.

Twelve teams competed in 2015's event. Each had 24 consecutive hours sometime during the month of May to find as many bird species as possible. No stranger to the Birdathon, Rob Ripma has competed several times, and was part of the winning team in 2015, seeing 164 species. It's all about timing, he says.

"If you're trying to get the best count, you're always shooting for the midpoint of May," Rob says. "Somewhere from May 18 to 22. For Indiana, that's the highest migration point to get the most species."

Rob and his brother Eric got involved in the Birdathon simply because they like doing big-day competitions. But it has come to mean more over the years.

"It's about what the money ends up helping to protect," Rob says.

That's true of most birdathons. Charity bird competitions help our feathered friends and their habitats thrive.

Bigger in Texas

Thanks to birds like this green jay, a Texas specialty, the cumulative species count for the Great Texas Birding Classic can reach 400.

Life in the Big City

Meet the urban dwellers of the bird world and find out how they're adapting to downtown life

by Kenn and Kimberly Kaufman

Even urban areas like New York City (pictured here) have good opportunities to see birds.

Peregrine falcons will nest on the tops of buildings.

WE'RE ALWAYS TELLING PEOPLE that "birds are everywhere." We say this especially when we're trying to convince them you can go bird-watching anywhere. And it's true. Birds *are* everywhere, from forests to prairies, from swamps to deserts to suburban yards. But can our metropolitan cities also serve as centers of bird life?

Actually, yes, they can! Surprising numbers of birds can be found even among the concrete and glass of our largest cities. Here are just a few examples of the birds that you might see among concrete jungles.

Adapting to Urban Lifestyles

When we think about city birds, some that come to mind first include pigeons, house sparrows and starlings. It makes sense that they would thrive in the city, because these are all birds imported from Europe. Over the course of many centuries, as European towns developed and grew into cities, these birds had time to adapt to the changes. When human settlers from Europe came to North America and started to build cities here, these imported birds had a head start over our native species.

House finches are common urban feeder birds.

Adaptability is the key, and many native North American birds are proving to be adaptable as well. One prime example is the house finch. Originally found in the western U.S. and Mexico, this colorful songster probably learned to live around the villages of the Hopi, the Navajo and other Native American people in the Desert Southwest. When the house finch was accidentally introduced into the New York area in 1940, it soon adapted to eastern cities and started to spread. The new eastern population met the expanding western flocks on the Great Plains in the 1990s, and today house finches are found in cities and towns from coast to coast.

Innovative Nesters

Some birds have very simple needs. They find their food in the air, so all they need is a place to build their nests. The chimney swift is a perfect example. It catches flying insects in high, swift flight, ranging for miles every day in search of airborne bugs. Centuries ago it built its nests in large hollow trees in the forest. Today, large hollow trees are harder to find, but every city has chimneys. The swifts use their sticky saliva to

These peregrine falcon chicks are on the roof of a Detroit high-rise. This species will often nest in cities.

Cliff swallows have adapted well to urban areas and can build a nest under almost any eave.

Many monk parakeets have escaped captivity and live in colonies. They often build nests on power lines, as this group did near Queens, New York.

paste a small platform of twigs to the inside of a chimney, creating a secure nest where they can lay their eggs.

Other aerial insect-eaters also find nesting sites downtown. The common nighthawk will lay its eggs directly on a gravel roof, where they are perfectly camouflaged. Cliff swallows will build their mud nests on the sides of buildings, but in more and more cities they are now placing those nests under bridges, where they are better protected from weather.

Even birds of prey find places to nest among the concrete canyons. The peregrine falcon, the world's fastest flying bird, will lay its eggs on ledges of skyscrapers in our largest cities. These urban peregrines often hunt high above the streets, chasing pigeons. In recent years, red-tailed hawks also have moved into cities, nesting

on buildings and hunting squirrels and sparrows in the local parks. The most famous urban red-tail, New York City's "Pale Male," has even been the subject of a book and a movie.

More New Kids in Town

In cities located along the shores of the ocean, lakes or large rivers, some birds take advantage of the specific habitat parking lots have to offer. They are favorite haunts of ring-billed gulls. Most kinds of gulls are opportunists anyway, and ring-bills are quick to adopt large open parking lots as places to rest, their flocks lining up and facing into the wind. Parking lots next to fast-food restaurants are especially popular, as the gulls can usually find choice leftovers dropped on the pavement.

At one time, crows and ravens were absent from American cities. Crows lived in wide-open

Common ravens (pictured) and crows have been moving into cities in recent decades.

nests on power poles or substations, and show up at bird feeders alongside sparrows and other less colorful creatures.

Temporary Guests

During much of the year, only a few of the most adaptable birds can be found downtown. But the sky's the limit during spring and fall migration seasons, because migrating birds may drop in anywhere. We have seen thrushes, warblers and other woodland species pausing among the skyscrapers in Boston, Philadelphia, Houston, Los Angeles and many other large cities. All they need are a tree or two to forage, and places to rest for their next flight. So keep your eyes open all the time, because birds really are everywhere!

farm country and ravens were mostly wilderness birds. They were often shot, and they had learned to avoid humans. But in recent decades, these intelligent and adaptable birds must have noticed that they weren't in danger when they ventured into suburbs and cities, so they moved right in. American crows now live in many cities from coast to coast, while common ravens thrive in some downtown areas of the West, like Phoenix and San Francisco. The stately raven of Poe's poem can even be seen perched on neon signs in Las Vegas.

One of the most surprising and colorful urban birds is the monk parakeet. With its shrill voice and bright green plumage, it seems out of place on our city streets—and it is, since it's native to South America, and was brought here as a cage bird. But in many parts of the U.S., monk parakeets have escaped from captivity, found each other and formed colonies. Dallas, Miami, Chicago and other big urban centers have thriving flocks of these flashy birds. They often build their bulky

6 Bird-Friendly Cities

While every city offers the chance to see some birds, a few of them have embraced birding in notable ways.

Portland, Oregon. From great blue herons living along rivers in town to swifts roosting in local chimneys, Portland finds ways to celebrate all kinds of urban birds.

New York City. America's biggest city hosts an astonishing variety of birds, especially in parks like Central Park, where organized bird walks are held almost every day in spring and fall.

Milwaukee, Wisconsin. Its location along Lake Michigan makes this a prime birding city all year. From ducks and gulls in winter to migrating hawks in fall and warblers in spring, there are always birds to see in Milwaukee's parks and nature centers.

Tucson, Arizona. Since 2001, Tucson has organized a citywide bird count every spring. Cactus wrens, verdins, curve-billed thrashers and other desert birds thrive even in the heart of town.

Austin, Texas. Austin is famous for live music and other cultural highlights, but it's also a hub of birding activity. Lakes and parks along the Colorado River bring abundant bird life to the city center.

St. Petersburg, Florida. Surrounded on three sides by the waters of Tampa Bay, the city teems with birds in all seasons, including pelicans, egrets, ospreys and more. Migration brings warblers and other songbirds to every park in town.

Flying High with Eagles

Though there are only two species in North America, eagles have won the hearts of birders everywhere

**by David Shaw
Fairbanks, AK**

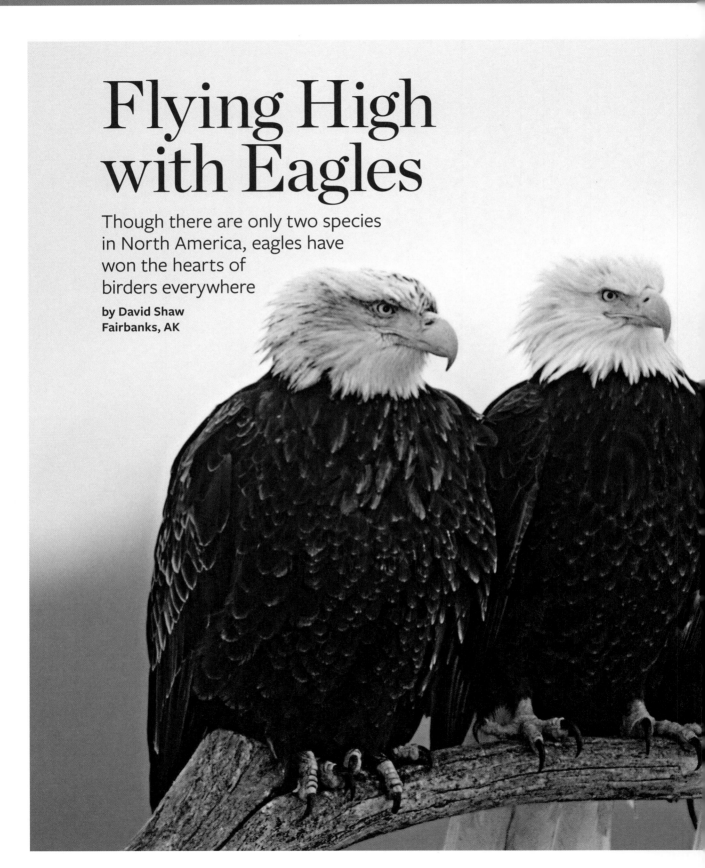

WAS 12, AND BOUNCING in nearly ecstatic excitement in the seat of the bright yellow school bus. The kids around me looked out the windows with mild interest, but I could hardly contain myself.

The winter oaks, bare of any leaves, allowed passing views of the gray water of the Susquehanna River. At what seemed a snail's pace, the bus pulled into the parking lot of the Conowingo Dam in northeastern Maryland. The driver shut down the engine with a sputter and, dreadfully slowly, finally opened up the bus's folding doors.

I bolted, flew up the bus aisle as though I were on wings, and bounded down the short steps to the asphalt below. "David! Wait!" called an adult from behind me. Ignoring the shout, I ran to the fence overlooking the river, my father's oversized binoculars bouncing dangerously around my neck. And there, just above me in the trees, was a bald eagle. No, wait—two, three, five, 10—too many to count. They were everywhere.

The winter sunlight filtering through the overcast sky lit up the white heads and tails of the adult birds and the scruffy mottled browns of the juveniles. They were huge, enormous, great hulking birds, eyeing the outflow of the dam with alert yellow eyes, waiting patiently for a fish to rise. For the first time since we'd left home that morning, I was speechless and still.

I've seen thousands of bald eagles since that day, from wintering birds in the wetlands of the Great Plains to congregations of hundreds around salmon streams in Alaska. I've watched them scrounge for garbage in city dumps, and delicately lift fish from lakes that looked like something on a postcard.

The diversity of places where bald eagles occur says something about the species. They are flexible—as happy eking out a living on what humans throw away as they are devouring fresh salmon from a wild river.

Bald eagles are found across North America in every state except Hawaii, almost always near water. Fish are an important part of their diet, but they are more often scavengers, eating carcasses, refuse or anything else into which they can sink their great yellow beaks.

This isn't to say they're not capable hunters. Bald eagles will happily catch mice, rabbits,

The enormous nests of bald eagles can weigh up to 2 tons!

Quick Facts
Eagles of North America

- Only two of the world's 61 eagle species live in North America.
- Bald eagles occur across the continent, mostly near water.
- Golden eagles live primarily in the West and North.
- Both species take five years to reach maturity.
- Subadult eagles (younger than 5 years) of both species can be age-identified by plumage characteristics.
- The bald eagle, the national symbol of the United States, was once threatened with extinction but is now recovering.

waterfowl, hares, seabirds, other raptors and even, on rare occasions, household pets. But their bread and butter comes in less attractive packaging.

Making a Comeback

Bald eagles nest exclusively off the ground, in trees or human-made structures. They build huge stick nests that a pair will use year after year to raise one to three chicks. The chicks, after fledging, take five years to fully mature, passing through a variety of plumages to reach the characteristic snow-white head and tail of the adults.

Though now abundant across most of their range, it was not so long ago that pesticide poisoning and persecution by humans hit bald eagles hard. Throughout the 19th century and the first half of the 20th, eagles were killed out of a misguided perception that they were competitors for fish and game. Then, in the mid-1900s, bald eagles took a second, even harder hit with the introduction of DDT to the environment.

By the mid-1960s there were fewer than 500 breeding pairs in the lower 48 states. As the cause of their decline became known and they became protected under the 1973 Endangered Species Act, they began to recover. Hunted and poisoned almost to extinction, the bald eagle now thrives over most of its former range. On June 29, 2007, the bald eagle was removed from the Endangered Species List, one of the major conservation victories of the past century.

Golden Touch

It was not until some years after my very first encounter with bald eagles on the Susquehanna that I came into a new kind of awe of the golden eagle, the great avian predator of the western mountains and deserts.

The first time I saw golden eagles it was as two distant spots through a pair of binoculars over the cliffs and sagebrush of the Snake River Birds of Prey area in Idaho.

In this area, as in most of their range, the eagles nest on cliff faces offering dramatic views of the surrounding landscape. Those two birds, soaring on an updraft, were too far away for me to appreciate in any real sense. That came later.

Goldens are as large as bald eagles but far more powerful. They fly with purpose, soaring in thermals and updrafts, carried high above the mountainous landscapes they call home.

Unlike bald eagles, goldens are not limited to North America. Their range extends across the three continents of the Northern Hemisphere. On ours, they occur mostly in the West and North. Migratory across the northern end of their range, they arrive in the early spring when the landscape is still covered in snow.

In Alaska, where I now live, they are harbingers of spring. Among the first migratory birds to arrive in the Alaska Range, they're eagerly awaited by birders and biologists alike.

Goldens avoided much of the havoc wrought by DDT, but that isn't to say they haven't suffered at the hands of humans. Even today, they are trapped and poisoned, usually accidentally, through much of the American West.

Filled with Passion

Golden eagles, while superficially similar to balds, are markedly different in power, prey and—dare I say?—passion. Their massive feet and talons can handle prey up to the size of deer, mountain sheep and caribou calves, though they only occasionally will take on such difficult prey. More often they feed on rabbits, hares, ground squirrels and a variety of birds up to the size of cranes and geese.

I mention passion because there is something about golden eagles. Perhaps it has to do with where they live: the sweeping deserts of the Southwest, the peaks of the Rockies and the glacier-clad mountains of Alaska. Or perhaps it is their size, speed, agility, grace and guts that make them seem so extraordinary and enduring.

Golden Beauty
As with bald eagles, it might take goldens a few years to fully develop the coloring on their heads. Below is a juvenile golden eagle.

Pseudo-Horns

Those "horns" on top of the great horned's head aren't ears at all, but feather tufts called plumicorns. Scientists theorize that owls use them to recognize each other.

The Greatest Hunter

Get an up-close look at the exciting lives of these fierce predators

by Sheryl DeVore

I F THERE'S A NESTING OWL in your neighborhood, there's a good chance it's a great horned. The second-largest owl species in North America, these birds of prey make themselves at home in a diverse range of habitats, including deserts, wetlands and forests.

Overall, they prefer woods near open areas and fields, but they aren't too picky about what they eat. From snakes and scorpions to rabbits and mice, a great horned owl's diet is expansive.

One thing that makes great horned owls skilled nocturnal hunters is their hearing capability. The owl's facial disk (the collection of feathers around the eyes) works like a satellite dish, trapping the sound and forcing it toward the ear canal. Its ears are on either side of the head, with one higher than the other to help the owl zero in on the location of its prey.

While fall and winter might seem like improbable times to nest, the great horned owl is no ordinary bird. "When the young are hatching, there has to be an abundant prey source to feed them, and great horned owls have it timed just right," says Jim Herkert, executive director of the Illinois Audubon Society. In late winter and early spring, plenty of mammals and other prey are available for the parents to bring to their recently hatched young.

Owls hoot at night, especially before breeding season in fall. A paired male and female utter a low series of five to eight hoots. They also bow to each other and rub their bills together. They raise their young in abandoned squirrel or hawk nests or in tree cavities. Females lay eggs in late November in Florida, late December in the Carolinas, and late January farther north.

The young hatch in about 30 days. The male brings food to his partner, who tears it into bite-sized pieces and feeds it to the young. In three weeks, their offspring begin peering out of the nest, showing off the white down on their heads. By seven weeks, fledgling great horneds make short flights, but adults continue to bring them food, responding to an eerie begging call that sounds like a human scream. Fledged owls typically stay with their parents for most of the summer.

Great horned owl numbers are declining, according to the Cornell Lab of Ornithology. To help, erect a wooden nesting platform with shallow sides in a live tree. Place large sticks and grass inside to mimic a hawk's or crow's nest. Once you've attracted a pair, listen for hoots in the autumn night. Just make sure you watch from a distance so you don't disturb them.

A Birthday Visitor

On the morning of her birthday, my wife was blessed with a gift from Mother Nature herself. The first thing Jan saw when she looked out the bedroom window was the neighborhood great horned owl gazing back at her! The bird continued to perch in the juniper tree for most of the morning.

Alan St. John
BEND, OR

Perfect Pairs

Great horned owl pairs are monogamous and may stay together for five years or more. Some researchers think they stick by each other's sides for life.

Stuff We Love

Award-winning photographer Paul Bannick takes readers along for the ride as he documents one year in the life of various owls in his book *Owl: A Year in the Life of North American Owls*. Visit barnesandnoble.com to order a copy.

Winged Giants by the Numbers

It's a numbers game when it comes to these heavy hitters

Bald eagle

98

Most young don't stay in the nest long, but it's a different story with larger birds such as owls, hawks and eagles. Bald eagles will stay in the nest up to 98 days!

ROLAND JORDAHL

25

At about 25 inches, the common merganser is one of the largest ducks in North America.

15

Ducks lay many more eggs than songbirds. For instance, wood ducks can lay as many as 15 eggs in one nesting cycle.

25,000

A small songbird usually has fewer than 4,000 feathers. A swan might have as many as 25,000.

5

Large birds need large nests! Bald eagle nests are about 5 to 6 feet in diameter and 2 to 4 feet tall. If the tree is strong enough, they will use the same nest again and again, adding new materials each year, so some nests can be enormous.

100

While on the hunt for prey, eagles can dive up to 100 miles per hour. But in regular flight, they can travel about 30 miles per hour.

20

If you hear loud noises in a forest, they might be coming from a turkey. These long-necked birds make more than 20 sounds, including the classic *gobble-gobble* produced by males. Some calls can be heard from a mile away!

I often take walks through Beaver Island State Park in Grand Island, New York. I am always in awe of the wildlife there—especially the great blue herons. There's usually a lot of heron action in the park in spring, thanks to a major rookery located on Pirates Island, on the Niagara River. I took this picture of one of the herons leaving an inlet, probably on its way back to the rookery after catching its lunch.

Caitlin Bozek
GRAND ISLAND, NY

One early spring morning, I noticed this Canada goose with her goslings sleeping comfortably underneath her wing. It was a particularly cool morning and her little ones needed warmth. I quickly grabbed my camera, hoping they wouldn't move a feather until I had a chance to capture the moment. I was thrilled to see mom and babies still snuggled in as I snapped this photo. I never knew Canada geese did this—so adorable!

Joanne Killmer
RINDGE, NH

My wife and I live on Bird Island, a small residential island in a 6,000-acre lake in central Florida. It's a designated bird sanctuary that is home to many waterfowl species. This photo shows one of the resident sandhill cranes. I photographed it and its mate from about 50 yards away, but this one crept closer to me until we were only 5 feet apart.

Wyatt Earp SUMMERFIELD, FL

The great gray owl is a rare, awe-inspiring sight in Yellowstone National Park. It was an honor to be in the presence of one of my favorite creatures and to capture an amazing image. I love that the owl is getting ready to take off—it seemed as if it posed just for me.

Danielle Kennedy HUNTINGTON STATION, NY

I took this picture in the fall at Shenandoah National Park in Virginia. As I was driving through the park, I noticed Ms. Turkey running toward me down a stone wall. It was such an amazing moment.

Ron Spratt
NOTTINGHAM, MD

I photographed this pileated woodpecker in Motley, Minnesota. It was an autumn day in the woods, and I liked the gold and yellow background of the fall leaves. The sun seemed to peek through the trees just enough to light up the woodpecker.

Colleen Gibbs
COON RAPIDS, MN

I'm lucky enough to live next to Versailles State Park, the second-largest state park in Indiana. This bald eagle was perched in a tree overlooking the lake, and I slowly worked my way to a spot directly below this amazing bird. It posed for about a half-hour and, from time to time, looked down to see what I was up to.

Jim Waldo
VERSAILLES, IN

Living in central Florida is fantastic! Our region has some of the most exciting and gorgeous bird species, like this osprey. As it swooped down to grab a fish, it stretched out its talons as it neared the water's surface, and I love how I was able to capture its pose at this exact moment.

TJ Waller
WINTER SPRINGS, FL

Two snowy white trumpeter swans were in the midst of a friendly fracas this particular winter day.

Cari Povenz, GRANDVILLE, MI